Come Search With Me

Let's Look for God

Subodh K. Pandit MD

DEDICATED
To
Mary Pandit

Words will not begin to tell how much you mean to me. Your constancy and love have guided me through life. You are the one person in whom is embodied the qualities I admire and cherish the most.

Ma, it is an honor and great joy to dedicate this book to you.

TABLE OF CONTENTS

PREFACE

I was born and brought up in India, a land with a rich and varied cultural heritage that goes back to 3000 BC, to the Indus Valley Civilization – one of the oldest known civilizations in history. The epochs contained in fifty centuries of cultural, political, religious, and military upheavals have made India what it is in this day and age. Today, it is a land teeming with a vast population of over a billion, who live amidst an amazing diversity of language, culture, food, dress, and religion. A few hours' journey by train can take you from a spot of familiarity to one that seems like a different country altogether.

It has the largest Hindu population in the world. The number of Muslims is the second largest of any country, and surpasses that in most Muslim countries themselves. Buddhism was born, cradled, and nurtured there. It flourished in the eastern regions before spreading out to the whole of Southeast Asia. Tradition has it that Christianity was brought to the peninsula by St. Thomas, one of Jesus' own disciples.

It arrived there, then, in its earliest nascent form. Sikhism and Jainism have their roots in that soil.

What a crucible of mixture! What an environment to grow up in! With shoulders rubbing in day-to-day encounters, the questions that sprang up were but natural and at times very troubling.

Yes, I did ask questions, many questions. So, let me take you on a journey of inquiry.

My journey.

It began innocuously – just mulling over the way people made religious claims. But once I decided to evaluate it for myself, it became a gripping adventure. For one thing, like the others, I too had made claims and had felt rather good about them. That is, till I did some honest introspection, when suddenly those claims did not seem all that convincing. The gap between the talk and the actual evidence was too big for comfort. There was a great deal of high sounding religious jargon but little else. I sensed that void and knew I had to address it. My challenging and yet exciting journey had begun.

The first questions I faced were deeply puzzling. I wanted to brush them aside and go on to more exciting themes; but try as I might, I just could not by-pass them. They were the simple, broad ones regarding life, religion and God that have been around for millennia and yet seem fresh to every generation. "What was life all about? Was there an ultimate purpose to it? How could anyone talk about a God they had never even seen? Did this God have an identity, like, maybe a name?"

Over the next twenty years I unobtrusively questioned as many people as I could and was amazed at the variety of answers I got. From the elite to the coarse; from the humble and hopeful to the proud and pretentious; from the blindly believing to the scornfully skeptical, the spectrum was wide indeed. Where and how was I to start the sifting process? Standing before such a myriad of voices, unable to decide whether to listen to just one voice, or the whole array, was a distressing dilemma.

More than that, my burning issue, what I really craved for, was solace. I longed for a safe, sturdy foundation to stand the times when the going got tough and I desperately needed explanations. For when those haunting questions began their relentless pounding, my meager knowledge was no match to withstand them. The answers did not become satisfactory just because they came from those I held in high esteem. Conviction, it seemed, could not be passed on passively either through the genes or as a contagion. I would have to struggle with each question myself. That foundation, to be stable and meaningful, would have to be personally and painstakingly laid.

But was there a foundation to be found? What if there was no such thing? Well then, I wanted to know that for myself. And if there was one, I felt compelled to find it.

I started out and soon realized that just a cursory glance, a half-hearted attempt, arbitrarily picking up a point here or there, would not do. I would have to be open to the full weight of evidence. If I was afraid of being proved wrong and even more afraid of having to make changes in my life, my quest was doomed even before it had begun. Of course being open and fair under such circumstances was easier said than done, yet I could not make that an excuse for not trying.

So, I made a choice – to start where the ground was level; taking the place of a common person 'on the street' and facing the myriad voices without my 'emperor's clothes' on. The dilemma notwithstanding, I felt I had made a beginning. But would I remain fair throughout? It was always a troubling thought, even though I knew that nobody on earth had risen completely free of bias and intolerance. I would just have to take it as a challenge and do my best.

So, now let's get on with this journey. If I prove to be an unworthy companion, the solution is simple – just drop the book. But if you agree that 'give and take' is integral to community life, respect and honesty can peacefully co-exist, and differing views need not spawn rancor or hostility, I invite you to COME SEARCH WITH ME. After-all, how pleasant and enjoyable can a journey get without fellow-travelers and companions!

INTRODUCTION

Every journey has unique features and if we look out for these attention-grabbers, the fascination they produce will hold the interest up the whole way. So, watch out for them; I think there will be enough to keep us from snoozing!

But first we need to prepare ourselves with two crucial things.

    A. Introspection
    B. Proper Atmosphere

[A] INTROSPECTION

Why do we need to examine ourselves? Because, unknown to us, we bring along a cartload of notions and ideas that can impede or divert us. Built up over the years, they cannot be rooted out easily, even when the stakes are high. How many peace-talks between the Palestinians and the Israeli's have broken down because of hatred and suspicion handed down from previous generations? Centuries after declaring, "All men are equal" people still cannot shake off their ingrained sense of superiority. We are prone to go by preset values that we are unwilling to change.

There's one particular attitude we need to be careful of. It is the pride in claiming to be open-minded. We like to be known as reasonable, balanced individuals. But we are seldom fair and unbiased. And here's where introspection is vital. We all have, blended in us, the mind of a believer, a skeptic and an inquirer, and can flit from one to the other so smoothly that we ourselves don't notice the change. The problem surfaces when we go straight to the believing or skeptical mode without going through the process of inquiry [all too common on the religious front]. Then when we are closely questioned or taunted regarding the basis of our beliefs, it comes as a shock that we cannot defend what we had taken for granted all along. We become confused and begin to question our own positions. This leads to greater confusion because the answers are not easily forthcoming. This vicious cycle can get so frustrating that some feel great relief in turning their backs on anything that has to do with religion. I can sympathize with that. If you are in such a state let me assure you that you are not alone. Some shelve their frustrations pretending everything is OK. Others silently wonder from where the right answers are going to come or if they will ever come! But take heart, all is not lost. It is to those who question and grope that our SEARCH will make the most sense and be the most rewarding.

I had mentioned three attitudes inherent in us. Let us try to describe them. Here are seven sets of statements to consider.

1) Skeptic – decides against a claim prior to thorough investigation
   Believer – decides to accept a claim prior to thorough investigation
   Inquirer – holds verdict till investigation is done

2) Skeptic – prefers those questions which introduce doubt
   Believer – prefers those questions which establish as fact
   Inquirer – asks questions mainly to gather information

3) Skeptic – focuses on the questions to the exclusion of the evidence
   Believer – focuses on the evidence to the exclusion of the questions
   Inquirer – focuses on the weight of evidence

4) Skeptic – disbelieves in the face of reasonable evidence
   Believer – believes in the face of big questions
   Inquirer – accepts reasonable evidence even if some questions remain

5) Skeptic – won't believe unless there is infallible proof

Believer – doesn't need any rational explanation for belief

Inquirer – willing to be swayed but only by evidence

6) Skeptic – unwilling to make counter-proposal – it might be disproved too

Believer – unwilling to make a counter-proposal – no need to

Inquirer – willing to evaluate both proposal and counter-proposal

7) Skeptic — the height of intellectual attainment is to ask – not expecting an answer

Believer – the height of faith is to remain unshakable no matter what

Inquirer – seeking a position of height not yet attained

During our sojourn, let us choose the attitude of an inquirer – one who holds verdict till the investigation is done. The believing and skeptical attitudes are so subtle that it will take frequent reminders to remain an inquirer throughout. But our first job is to make the choice.

[B] ATMOSPHERE

Numerous attempts to scale Mt. Everest [at 29,028 ft, the highest mountain peak in the world] had to be abandoned. The swinging, unpredictable atmospheric conditions — wind, temperature, ice, visibility etc. would suddenly become mean and menacing, forcing the climbers to turn back and give up in frustration — another attempt aborted despite all the meticulous and expensive preparations. It might have been different if the surrounding conditions had not become so harsh and hostile.

Fortunately, for our journey, the conditions are not entirely out of our control. We can choose and maintain the atmosphere that will surround us. But to create such an atmosphere, we will need the following: (1) Humility (2) Honesty (3) Calmness and (4) Respect. We must pave our road with them, taking care to see that none is overlooked or discarded because the absence of even one will severely hamper us.

I. Humility

This is of utmost importance and is irreplaceable. All the other factors are secondary to it. Some tend to think of it negatively as a groveling, self-depreciating posture; but humility is not concerned about a public image. It is not something put on. Rather, it springs up and grows as we contemplate the vastness, beauty and grandeur of truth. Even without defining it, we know from deep within that it is unimaginably great and awe-inspiring. All who have reflected on it have been compelled to a sense of sacredness and reverence. How small we feel in its presence! And that forms the true basis of humility.

We can also realize it on a lesser scale as we appreciate the wealth of knowledge in those around us. It effectively leads away from pride and arrogance to an attitude of learning. The mind is mellowed to become open and accepting.

Nothing can be as important as humility in our search.

II. Honesty

This is a scarce commodity! I've met with all kinds of cover-ups, pretenses and 'white lies'; anything, just to avoid the appearance of ignorance. I've also come across a peculiar notion which holds that if we are strongly convinced about something, our enthusiasm and passion should be accepted as sufficient evidence of its validity. An impartial inquiry is not required and honesty can be put aside as long as we are defending what we feel honor-bound to defend. This has become so much a part of us that it will take more than an ordinary effort to recognize and reject it. One way is to make a definition of honesty that is sharp, clear, with 'teeth' in it and then rigorously apply it. Here is such a definition: "Honesty is the willingness to accept and acknowledge the value of a point or argument, no matter who brings it to the table, even if that affirmation has the possibility of destroying my own previous stand." I call it the "Wow Factor". If a point or piece of information is impressive, we should be willing to let it amaze us. We should be willing to say, "Wow!" and mean it, rather than first consider the implications and acknowledge only what is 'safe' – only that which will support our position and belief. But that would be unfair. We should be prepared to go where the evidence leads.

To inquire seriously is to inquire honestly.

III. Calmness

Back in 1879 after more than a thousand experiments, Thomas Alva Edison finally succeeded in inventing and producing the electric bulb. The challenge had been to find the right balance between heat and light in the delicate filament inside. In scores of experiments, either the filament would not glow sufficiently, or just when it did, it got too hot and burned off the contact points.

Religious discussions also require a balance. They can get dull and stereotyped and end in complete apathy, or become so vitriolic and bitter that broken relationships, enmity and even war can result.

Calmness is keeping our volatile emotions in check because we recognize it to be in line with humility and honesty. It is a choice we make so that the matter at hand can be evaluated fairly. If we are not humble and honest, emotions are bound to get out of hand and once they do, they instantly dominate and sever the contact with reason and judgment. The conclusions will be anything but correct and fair. Whereas if we stay calm and balanced, the contact will be preserved; and light, meaning wisdom and understanding, will have a chance to glow.

Calmness makes sure that the light stays on.

IV. Respect

Many think that respect automatically implies agreement. It does not. In fact, it shines out best when there is disagreement. We also tend to use it as a synonym for admiration. But it is not necessarily so.

Respect is to allow for the other person whatever rights we claim for ourselves. Whatever freedom we use in making our choices, we freely grant to the others – even if their choice is totally against our personal values. Mutual respect means that we ourselves are granted that same freedom by the others out there.

Respect will never allow us to look down our noses at those who differ from us and call them names, hurl insulting epithets, slip in damaging insinuations or condescendingly pity them. To be able to respectfully disagree is a virtue and will, in turn, bring respect even from critics and antagonists.

Respect will bring credibility to our findings.

Humility, honesty, calmness and respect appear a strong foundation. But how do we make a practical application? The first step is to join the person ' on the street' – one who has no loyalty to any particular religion or philosophy.

During the seminars I present, we go through a little ritual to symbolize this. The attendees stand up, draw an imaginary circle round their feet and then step out of that circle signifying letting go of those philosophies. Of course it is only a ritual. Nobody can abandon deep-seated ideas in just a moment. The meaning is not to discard them altogether, but to refrain from rising up in passionate defense of them. Our inclination to pride, dishonesty and emotional outbursts will lose its grip on us because what we wanted to defend has been laid aside. We now have no bone to pick, no ax to grind. There is a freedom this brings that is vital to a search such as ours.

Let us accept and genuinely desire to implement them, and they will provide the atmosphere that will take us the distance. No guarantees – just the best chance.

CHAPTER I

THE EXISTENCE OF GOD

"Allah ho Akbar", proclaims the Muslim cleric from the highest minaret of his mosque, sending those words to the farthest corners of his community. "Allah" is the proper name of God in Arabic. "Ho Akbar" means "is great". What he really means to say is that Allah is greater than any other. With these words he exhorts the faithful, at the appointed hour, to 'salat' [prayer], one of the five fundamental pillars of the Islamic faith.

"Shema Israel", intones the Jewish rabbi, with a kippur on his head and the tallic [ceremonial shawl] around his shoulders. He is in the presence of the sacred Torah, the Books of Law in which is recorded the words that Moses got directly from Jehovah on Mt. Sinai. "Adonai Elohenu, Adonai achhod". "Hear O Israel, the Lord, the Lord our God is one".

"Om mani padme hum", recites the Tibetan Buddhist monk, while his Japanese counter-part repeats, "Namo Amitabh, Namo Amitabh". The Tibetan's mantra is one of the most sacred, "O the jewel in the Lotus". The Japanese chants the "Name of Amitabh" a bodhisatva [one who has reached the penultimate state – just before attaining Buddha hood] who presides over the Pure Land Paradise.

"There is no other name under heaven", thunders the Christian preacher/pastor, "given among men by which we must be saved". The name he refers to is Jesus of Nazareth, the son of Mary, who was called the "Christ", meaning the Anointed One, the Messiah. He was also called "Immanuel" which means "God with us".

Deep in the Indian peninsula, a guru and his shishya's [followers/students], saffron-robed and with shaved heads, break into a chant while on a pilgrimage, "Hare Krishna, Hare Krishna, Krishna, Krishna, Hare, Hare. Hare Rama, Hare Rama, Rama, Rama, Hare, Hare". Rama is the seventh avatar [incarnate] and Krishna the eighth, of the God Vishnu, the Preserver of the universe.

Widespread and diverse – this religious world!

On the other side of the fence stands the rank skeptic, the avowed atheist. With a wry smile on his face he condescendingly taunts, "O these poor deluded souls. How utterly futile to sip at 'the opium of the masses'"! For that is what Karl Marx had called religion. He felt that those who believed in religion and God were just using them as props and crutches to hobble through life, hoping to deaden the sense of pain and suffering which formed the reality of life. And what was more, this life was utterly purposeless. All claims of heaven and a utopia somewhere out there had been brought in because of the inability to face the naked truth of our present aimless existence. There was no God, no after-life, no heaven. Nobody knew where we came from, or where we were going.

Was this the 'reality' that everyone else had missed? Bertrand Russell a brilliant, British atheistic philosopher, in an essay,[1] giving his reason for refusing to become a believer, said, that it is "only on the firm foundation of unyielding despair that the soul's habitation can henceforth be safely built". I immediately felt the clash of ideas in that sentence. For how could 'despair' form a firm foundation; and how could 'unyielding despair' ever be 'safe'?

Quentin Smith, another atheist, and co-author of Theism, Atheism and The Big Bang Cosmology was blunt, "... the only reasonable belief is that we came from nothing, by nothing and for nothing". And what was such a bold, sweeping claim based on? The only reasonable answer I could come to was, 'Nothing'! It was as wild a guess as any I had ever come across. If the base was 'nothing' it could uphold nothing and Russell's 'unyielding despair' probably was founded on this nothingness. But nothingness and emptiness is not an easy philosophy to live by. It is a hard, unrewarding principle. No wonder Jean Paul Sartre, the French thinker and philosopher, after waxing eloquent on his well-structured arguments for discarding the notion of the supernatural and God, confessed that the only question that remained was why he had not committed suicide! The 'nothingness' of Smith will force one towards the 'unyielding despair' of Russell and ultimately drag the soul to the precipice of Sartre. Such is the depth that these despairing philosophies and questions can drive us to.

But just because somebody was despairing and wanted to commit suicide did not make it wrong. I knew of religious and pious people, who also wanted to commit suicide. Merely shooting out labels and libels at one side or the other, would not do. The underlying question had not yet been answered — the question of whether or not God existed. It had to be faced squarely first. What use looking for a named river or lake if the existence of water itself was in question?

Is there a God in existence?

To this question there can be only two answers. The response of those who say they do not know and cannot decide, is not an answer. It could be a confession of ignorance on their part or a claim regarding paucity of knowledge on the subject; but it is not an answer to the question.

The two answers are:

1) 'God' is non-existent, fictitious.
2) God exists and is factual.

The claims are irreconcilable and mutually exclusive. I call it the Great Divide.

"The universe we observe has *precisely* the properties we should expect if there is, at bottom, no design, no purpose, no evil and no good, nothing but blind, pitiless indifference." [2]

"... the seemingly arbitrary and unrelated constants in physics have one strange thing in common – these are *precisely* the values you need if you want to have a universe capable of producing life. ... there is no good reason for an intelligent person to embrace the illusion of atheism or agnosticism." [3]

Notice how both the statements use the word "precisely" claiming to refer to 'facts' that they say are freely available. Something had to have gone awry if both were referring to facts and yet making diametrically opposing and mutually exclusive claims.

One factor I think, is the way the debate is structured. Each side makes claims for itself and then challenges the other to disprove them or make better claims themselves. The drawback to this type of thinking is the tendency to come to conclusions by default. If I showed good evidence for my side then by default the other side could not; or if I showed the other side's claim to be deficient then by default mine was established. But on looking over the scene I found that there was enough support for each side to think to stake their claims and enough deficiencies to keep either side from making dogmatic, silly [meaning unsubstantiated] statements. I have heard believers mockingly describe apes and monkeys as the ancestors of unbelievers, without realizing that it would apply to them too. I have read atheists who propound the ' Scientific Law' of evolution, without giving a second thought whether the word 'law' would stand scrutiny. Neither of these is true and neither statement impressed me. I wanted the 'facts' to make up my own mind.

So, I drew up what I called the *Pan Process, which I hoped would keep me in the mode of inquiry. The principle simply put: When there are two mutually exclusive options, the tendency is to build two columns of arguments; one, showing the positive points for your side and the other showing the negative points of the opposing side. This is good as a defense for what one has already established. But the Pan Process, a process of inquiry, requires four columns— two columns for each option – one for [pro] and one against [con].

Once the four columns are filled we can step back and see if the weight of evidence tilts the balance one way or the other.

*Note: Pan stands for
[1] going across boundaries, scanning the whole horizon as in the Pan- American Games.
[2] the process of sifting; like a person who pans for gold; separating the valuable from the ordinary.
[3] the first three letters of my family name Pandit.

THE PAN PROCESS

Proposal [A] – God is non-existent, fictitious

Column One:

Arguments for option [A].

There are none! Surprised? But it's true. This is because the statement is a negative one. A negative statement is valid when, and *only when*, all the possibilities have been exhausted. If I claimed that there were 10,000 lakes in the USA and none of them was named Chargoggagogg manchauggagoggchaubunagungamuagg*, how many lakes would I have to be familiar with? All 10,000. Even 9,999 will not be sufficient to establish that claim.

*Note: There is such a lake in Massachusetts. It is the longest name in the USA and is in the Native American language. Translated, it says, "You fish on your side of the lake; I fish on my side and nobody fishes in between!"[4]

Let's apply this to just one factor regarding God, His location. He could be residing anywhere in the universe. None of us can claim to know every nook of the town in which we live, much less the country, or the world, or the moon, or the solar system, or the Milky Way galaxy with its one hundred billion stars, or the one hundred and twenty-five billion galaxies estimated by the astronomers. By what stretch of imagination can a human claim to be familiar with all that! And it isn't as if we've looked at most of the places and only a few now remain to be checked out – rather, what we do know compared to what is unknown is so little as to be counted closer to zero than any number. Even if we had checked out 99% of the universe, we would still have more than one billion galaxies left to be inspected!

Furthermore, this God could probably move about. If you went looking for Him in Canada, He could have gone to India. To make a valid claim then, we should know every spot in the universe and be everywhere at the same time. This is called omniscience and omnipresence. They are the characteristics attributable only to God. So, to exhaust all the possibilities and thus prove that there is no God in existence, one has to possess the attributes of God or become a God himself! The tangled knot is evident.

There are no arguments in this column.

Column Two:

Arguments against [B]. I believe there are four such arguments.

[1] The lack of empirical evidence.
[2] The presence of pain, suffering, cruelty.
[3] The lack of design or the presence of bad design
[4] Difficulty with 'creation'.

[1] Lack of Empirical Evidence
Empirical evidence is a direct form of knowledge like seeing and touching and tasting for your-

self. I have never seen or heard God, like I do other humans. This confession could imply that there is no God. But there are so many other entities that I have never seen or felt and yet have believed in their existence, like, my own brain or the chemical formula for water. They constitute reality to me and to everyone else I know. The majority of scientific deductions fall into this category. I do agree with the observation that many who say that they have heard God cannot provide evidence for it. So, yes, empirical evidence is missing and that could be an argument, but it is a weak one at best.

[2] The Presence of Pain, Suffering, Cruelty

This is a fairly strong argument because of the claim that God is good and kind. Darwin struggled trying to reconcile the idea of a good God with the cruelty he saw in nature. However, thinking closely, it is not an argument against the existence of God but against the kind of God being described. In other words, if some of these questions were satisfactorily answered and He was found to be good and kind after all, He could very well be in existence. Or, He could be just a bad God, but in existence all the same.

There is another question that arises. Pain and suffering do not constitute the whole spectrum of our experiences. Exquisite pleasures and deep joys are also to be found. If pain and suffering point to the absence of God, what do such joys and pleasures indicate? To be fair they should point to the presence of God. So, at best, these observations nullify each other.

[3] Lack of Design or Presence of Bad Design

Firstly, the argument need not refer to non-existence, rather, to something not done adequately or in the right manner by this God. It could actually be a subtle confession of His existence.

Secondly, there is design all around us, myriads of them. They are not simple like a wooden toy car, but are complex, intricate and extremely precise. Yes, there are areas that appear chaotic and disorderly, but if these suggest the absence of God, then what do the millions of mind-boggling designs point to? A broken vase is still a vase. To point to only the jagged, broken edge and claim complete lack of design in the whole structure is false reasoning. Chaos in one area does not change design at another point to anything other than design. If there is both design and randomness in the same structure, it is the design that takes precedence and provides the correct feature of that structure even if present in small measure. But it is not present in just small measure in nature. It is overwhelming in extent. What appears to be lack of design and bad design shrink into insignificance in the face of the magnitude and precision of design all around us. It would be unscientific and untruthful to ignore this.

[4] Difficulty with Creation

There were two problems I faced when trying to explain creation.

One, it is not something that has been observed.
Two, it is not in conformity to any known law of
nature or science.

Thus to the rational mind which invariably seeks
an explanation, to simply claim that it happened in
a particular manner is not at all satisfying. *Creatio
ex nihilo* [creating something out of nothing] does
not appeal to reason. The dependence on belief/faith
is obvious and has to be conceded. But if this is not
acceptable, is there another explanation that is superior, where scientific evidence and logic take the
place of this take-it-or-leave-it type of story? Will a
completely random and totally undirected, unsuper-
vised event such as the Big Bang of Singularity fit
the bill? More of this later.

In the Newtonian type of approach, appealing to
a known law would have been a strong argument.
But after the questions raised by quantum physics
and the relativity of Einsteinian thinking, we know
we are at a loss to explain, let alone enunciate a law
regarding, all what we observe. Therefore something
that does not fit into our present repertoire of knowledge need not be the basis of making final conclusions regarding such huge, all-encompassing ideas
like the presence or absence of God.

Proposal [B] – God exists; is factual

Column Three:

Arguments for option [B]

[1] Circumstantial Evidence

(a) Sheer Numbers

If just one person told me that there was a calf with a head attached to both ends of the body, I would easily dismiss the report. If five hundred people testified to it, I may not believe it right away, but I would give it a second thought. If a million said the same thing, my response would shift from disbelief to there being a good possibility that such an outlandish creature did really exist.

Billions believe in the existence of God and are willing to testify to that from personal experience. It is reasonable to shift from disbelief to there being a possibility of the claim.

(b) Deep In Human Psyche

From the dawn of human history, there has never been a single generation that did not believe in the existence of the supernatural. If an idea has stayed around for a century, it should lend a measure of credibility to it. If it persists for thousands of years in the hearts of millions and billions, in an unbroken chain till today, it becomes a form of evidence that is difficult to disregard.

(c) Presence Of Design

Every scientific discovery, whether in the subatomic sphere or in the gigantic world of astrophysics, has shown in greater and yet greater force the overwhelming presence of design in the very structure of nature and the universe.

Why is it that we never hear of an archeologist [an acknowledged scientist] who unearths an ornate pillar from the rubble and then declares, "It happened by itself. Nobody made it. I never saw the one who could have done it."? How come he was able to differentiate it from the dirt around it? Because there was a design in the pillar and none that was obvious in the dirt. Now, what if there is design in the matter that makes up dirt? Shouldn't a scientist acknowledge that and go looking for the maker of that matter just like he went looking for the maker of the pillar?

Why would a jury not accept a story from a defendant that described a gun coming out of its case from the closet and turning and firing at the victim ' all by itself'? Nobody saw the person who did it anyway!

The most die-hard skeptic will not accept such ideas. They will be dismissed even before they are stated. Why? Because a design or a purposeful act demands the presence of a person, a mind behind it.

All the manufacturing units in the world put together, would not equal the complexity, intricacy and precision of even one system like the nervous system in our bodies. And there are multiple systems in us; and multiplied numbers in the animal and plant world and in the universe, all working together with an uncanny co-ordination. Sure, it is not proof of the existence of God, but it is powerful evidence of a mind out there. Why would anyone propose the idea that they all happened by themselves?

[2] Logical Analysis

(a) The Kalam Argument. Al Ghazali, a Muslim, who lived in the eleventh century CE, formed a simple three step deduction.

Step one – Anything that begins has a cause.
Step two – This universe has a beginning.
Step three – Therefore the universe has to have a cause.

(b) The 'Pan' Argument. Three steps again.

Step one – 'Scientists' claim that matter, energy, space and time are the only entities in the universe. Nothing else exists. Nothing is supernatural.
Step two – The cause of a substance or product lies outside, and is transcendent to, the substance/product. For instance, the wooden table cannot be the cause of the wooden table; nor can we say that wood is the cause of that table. The carpenter could be the cause but he is distinct from the substance/product.
Step three – Therefore we cannot appeal to matter, energy etc as the cause of matter, energy etc. The cause must be distinct from the substance. The Cause has to be supernatural.

This Cause must possess at least two characteristics that should conform to what we observe in nature. Firstly, material nature in the vast universe of 125 billion galaxies is complex and intricate to an overwhelming degree. The Cause therefore can be deduced to possess an ability of immense proportions – a giant intellect that was able to conceive, execute and keep tab on the whole multifaceted structure. Albert Einstein described his "rapturous amazement at the harmony of natural law, which reveals an intelligence of such superiority that, compared with it, all the systematic thinking and acting of human beings is an utterly insignificant reflection".[5]

Second, the energy involved in the universe is of a magnitude beyond our comprehension. The Cause must at least match that in inherent power and be able to control it sufficiently to focus on a subatomic particle on the one hand, as well as provide energy for the mightiest cluster of galaxies on the other.

A giant intellect possessing immense energy could refer to something like God. There is nothing to preclude such a conclusion.

[3] Anthropic Principle

This term was coined in 1973 by a British scientist Brandon Carter and describes the factors that probably started and maintain life on planet earth.

These factors are so many and so precise that a spontaneous, random cause is extremely unlikely.

"Take the expansion rate of the universe which is fine-tuned to one part in a trillion, trillion, trillion, trillion, trillion, trillion. That is, if it were changed by *one part* in either direction – a little faster, a little slower – we could not have a universe that would be capable of supporting life".[6]

"Gravity has an incomprehensibly narrow range for life to exist".[7]

"When you combine the two [gravity and cosmological constant] the fine-tuning would be to a precision of one part in a hundred million trillion, trillion, trillion, trillion, trillion, trillion. That would be the equivalent of *one atom* in the entire known universe!"[8]

"... the original phase-space volume required fine tuning to an accuracy of one part in ten billion multiplied by itself one hundred and twenty-three times ... would require more zero's than the number of elementary particles in the entire universe!"[9]

Let's look at another factor – our location in space. "It is only in the inner edge of the Circumstellar Habitable Zone where you can have low enough carbon dioxide and high enough oxygen to sustain complex animal life. And that's where we are."[10]

"We happen to be situated safely between the Sagittarius and Perseus spiral arms... I really can't come up with an example of another place in the galaxy that is as friendly to life as our location"[11]

And we have not even scratched the surface of the number of factors of this kind. [Examples: The sun being the right mass, with the right ratio of colored light, the right composition, the right distance, the right orbit, the right galaxy, the right location; the structure of the solar system with specific features of our moon and of the planets; the earth itself with its location, size, composition, atmosphere, temperature, internal dynamics, many intricate cycles like the carbon cycle, oxygen cycle, nitrogen cycle, phosphorus cycle, sulfur cycle, calcium cycle etc. — all to nurture living organisms on a circling planet.[12]

"Over the past thirty years or so, scientists have discovered that just about everything about the basic structure of the universe is balanced on a razor's edge for life to exist."[13]

Another consideration is regarding the fact that we, on planet earth, are peculiarly positioned to make scientific observations. Ours is the only location in the universe from where a total solar eclipse can be viewed and experienced. This has allowed scientific studies of the color spectrum of the sun which would not have been possible otherwise. It has helped establish the only observable part of the Theory of

Relativity which states that gravity can bend light. It also provides a historical record of changes in the earth's rotation. The sun is four hundred times the size of the moon and is exactly four hundred times the distance. The area they occupy in the sky is exactly equal, one to the other. "It's that incredible coincidence that creates a perfect match."[14]

> "Our location away from the galaxy's center and in the flat plane of the disc provides us with a particularly privileged vantage point for observing both nearby and distant stars."[15]

> "The very composition of our atmosphere gives it transparency"[16]

> "To find that we have a universe where the very places where we find observers are also the very best over-all places for observing – *that's* surprising. I see design ... in this very pattern of habitability and measurability."[17]

This would be like going to the control room at the Kennedy Space Center just before final countdown and finding every one of the hundreds and thousands of dials at exactly the precise point necessary for the success of the whole venture from the initial planning to the safe return of the space shuttle, and then claiming that it all happened by sheer coincidence! Yet, even this illustration pales in comparison with what we observe in nature. To place every one of the thousands of needles at the only point in each dial so as to originate and perpetuate life, requires a master control center. To me, any other explanation would be far inferior to this and leave more questions unanswered.

[4] Instant Formation of Granite

Granite is said to be the primordial rocks of the earth, formed over geological time scales of multiplied millions of years. The elements then present, were subjected to certain ranges of temperatures and pressure, to gradually synthesize the rocks that we see all over the world today.

But discoveries from the famous Oak Ridge Laboratory in Tennessee, USA, which were published in standard and prestigious international scientific journals, tell a completely different story.

Polonium 218 [Po-218] is a radio isotope without an earlier form [precursor] and has a known half life of three minutes. The radiation causes a signature halo in the particles of rock during the decay of the isotope. Any substance, then, that has captured a halo, had to do it in three minutes or less.

It has been incontrovertibly demonstrated that granite rocks from around the world including the gigantic El Capitan and Half Dome Rock in Yosemite National Park, California, contain Polonium 218 halos in such quantity as to establish the wide spread nature of the phenomenon. The scientific deduction is astounding – those giant rocks, that seem to make up the foundation and framework of the crust of planet earth, were formed in three minutes![18]

Nobody has yet formed a piece of granite in the laboratory using the theorized raw materials and the temperatures and pressures proposed – suggesting that the theory should be open to question. Nobody has yet demonstrated an original fossil embedded in granite rock – suggesting that there was no extended period of time involved in the process.

I met Dr. Gentry personally in April 2008 in Maryland, USA where he clearly stated that nobody had yet successfully challenged [disproved] these significant findings.

Therefore, till such time as they are shown to be false, we have no option but to accept the present scientific conclusion that the event – formation of granite – most likely took place in three minutes, and not millions and millions of years. The personal opinions of big wigs in scientific circles cannot make this more or less than a scientific fact based on the best evidence to date.

As inquirers we should rely on evidence, not opinions and unfounded theories. However wrong the "three-minute" claim may ultimately turn out to be, the scientific inquirer inside of us should not bow to any but the best available, reasonably established, information of today.

Column Four:

Arguments against [A]

Statistical Analysis.

'Chance' is a subjective idea that we all use every day in making a host of decisions. It is also a mathematical tool called probability. The relevant numbers are plugged into the formula and the result gives us an indication whether it might or might not occur.

In day-to-day life we can say that an event that has only one chance of occurrence in 10^8 [100 million] is considered an impossibility; and 10^8 chances of occurrences to one of non-occurrence as fact. In scientific evaluations the number goes up to 10^{15} [quadrillion]. When it comes to stating a scientific law, we are told that the number is 10^{50}. In other words if there is a mathematical probability of something occurring 10^{50} times, with only one chance of failure, the event is said to have been established as a law, meaning it will always occur. Conversely, if there is only one chance of occurrence and 10^{50} chances of failure, the event is considered to be utterly impossible.

Of course these numbers are arbitrary. But they are too huge to question. How big are these numbers anyway? Let me try to illustrate. Suppose I wanted to test gravity by dropping a ball from my hand once every second, looking for that one chance when it will not come down but will stay suspended or simply float away. To test it 10^{18} times, it will take me 15 billion years. That is the age of the universe according to the Big Bang theory. If I wanted to test it 10^{20} times it would take 1.5 trillion years — 100 times the age of the entire universe! So, 10^{50} is admittedly arbitrary but it is an astronomical figure, too huge to question. One chance, then, in 10^{50} is stating an utter impossibility.

Dr. Michael Denton[19] is considered one of the first to statistically challenge Darwin's idea of spontaneous generation of life. He looked at the simplest cell that could possibly live and function. What were the chances that one hundred proteins [the smallest number required] could come together by sheer coincidence? His calculation showed a probability of one in 10^{2000}! Remember that 10^{50} is an impossibility. Now, let's just suppose there was a colossal mistake in the calculation and the real number should be smaller by a factor of 100 billion. That would be quite a blunder for a scientist to make, but let's just say he did. What is 10^{2000} divided by 100 billion? Precisely 10^{1989}. We've hardly made a dent in it! So, it is futile to question these numbers with a skeptical attitude.

Ralph Muncaster[20], in his book ' A Skeptic's Search For God' stated that the chances of getting 10,000 amino acids with left-sided links [which is absolutely necessary], and 100,000 nucleotides with right-sided links [again absolutely necessary] together in one cell, was one in $10^{33,113}$!

Harold Morowitz[21] calculated the odds of a whole cell randomly assembling under the most ideal circumstances to be one in $10^{100,000,000,000}$ [100 hundred billion]! How about a "WOW"!! To just write the zero's down at one per second will take more than 3170 years! And we have not computed the other factors in, like the exact function of each molecule, division of that cell, increasing biological complexity, life from some unknown source injected into the organism, plant life, animal life, human life with such abstract qualities as love, courage, honesty etc. If the list itself is endless, what would the combined chances be for all the components to come into existence and then come together spontaneously, by sheer coincidence? Statistically, an absolute impossibility!

And here's some logic attached to the numbers: If there are two mutually exclusive options [A] and [B], only one of which is correct, then;

if [A] is possible so is [B];

if [A] becomes improbable, [B] becomes probable;

if [A] is shown to be impossible, [B] becomes fact!

For example, if I asked what the square root of 25 was and gave you two options only one of which was right; then proposed 33 as the first option, but refused to disclose the other, which would you choose? The second hidden option, of course, even if you never set eyes on it, because the square root of a whole number greater than one is always smaller than the number. The first option of 33, being greater than 25, made it impossible. This makes option two the right answer. Strangely and yet significantly, you don't have to even see the second one to make that choice. It will still be the correct one.

If the formation of that first cell was utterly impossible by random chance, reason demands that we accept the only other explanation – that it was a supervised process/event.

Let's put the columns together.

God, non-existent	column one: No arguments
	column two: They raise questions but are not strong conclusions.
God, factual	column three: Circumstantial evidence, logical analysis, the anthropic principle and Granite formation together form a fairly strong argument.
	column four: Statistical Analysis – spontaneous generation statistically impossible.

It appeared a fair evaluation and the weight of evidence was difficult to deny. The balance was tilted decisively.

> "... the absolutely overwhelming evidence points toward an intelligence behind life's creation"[22]

> "The universe is unlikely, very unlikely. Deeply, shockingly unlikely".[23]

"Science you might say has discovered that our existence is infinitely improbable and hence a miracle"[24]

Why do scientists continue to disbelieve in the existence of God? I cannot answer for all of them but there appear to be factors other than scientific ones.

"...they're not excited because they disagree with the science; it's because they see the extra-scientific implications ... they don't like where it's leading"[25]

"For a fruitful debate we need to understand evolution's foundation... We need to understand this because ultimately evolution is not about scientific details. Ultimately evolution is about God."[26]

"Spontaneous generation was disproved one hundred years ago, but that leads us to only one other conclusion, that of super-natural creation. We cannot accept that on *philosophical* grounds; therefore we *choose* to believe the impossible: that life arose spontaneously by chance."[27]

Others have been rather forthright. "I didn't want there to be a God, who would hold me responsible for my immoral lifestyle"[28]

"Why should God rule and I serve?"[29]

"I don't want there to be a God; I don't want the universe to be like that".[30]

How do evolutionary scientists describe the origins of the universe and life?

"Singularity has no 'around' around it. There is no space for it to occupy, no place for it to be .. There is no past for it to emerge from. And so, from nothing, our universe begins. In a single blinding pulse ... the singularity assumes heavenly dimensions, space beyond conception.... So, what caused it? ... some quality or thing, that introduced a measure of instability into the nothingness that was."[31]

This is supposed to be a scientific explanation! What is the basis of such unfounded statements? "The laws of physics do not exist in a singularity"[32] So, Bryson was free to state what was not in line with natural scientific laws.

And how did life start? "It was a singularly hostile environment and yet somehow life got going. Some tiny bag of chemicals twitched and became animate. We were on our way."[33]

Now, really, is this an explanation at all? How is this different from the "difficulty with Creation" we had faced earlier? Nobody has ever observed this and it does not conform to any known scientific law.

In the borrowed words of Henry Gee, Chief Science Writer for Nature (1999): It is "...an assertion that carries the same validity as a *bedtime story* – amusing, perhaps even instructive, but not scientific".[34]

Misia Landau author of Narratives Of Human Evolution was struck by the similarity between accounts of human evolution and *old fashioned folk tales*.[35]

".. the materialistic views of Darwin, Huxley, Simpson, Monod and Dawkins are based on personal philosophy, not empirical evidence ... this is not science but *myth*"[36]

"... almost impossible for the non-scientist to discriminate between the legitimately weird and the *outright crackpot*"![37]

It would not be reasonable or fair to heap scorn on the 'naive' faith of those who believe in the 'magic' of creation and then propose a 'magical' event without even a magician being present! I wonder which requires more of this 'naive' faith.

I agreed with a statement made [on another topic] by George Hanson[38], "The difficulties of belief may be great; the absurdities of unbelief are greater". I chose to believe.

See Page 173, Appendix I, for my discussion on Ultimate Purposelessness.

REFERENCES

1. Bertrand Russell, Why I Am Not a Christian, 1957, p106
2. Richard Dawkins, Oxford Biologist in Science 277, 1997
3. Patrick Glynn in God: The Evidence, 1997
4. Russell Ash, Top 10 of Everything, Dorling Kindersley Ltd., 2000, p88
5. Mircea Eliade, Ed. The Encyclopedia of Religion, p322
6. Stephen Meyer, a philosopher whose field of study was the history of molecular biology, the history of physics and evolutionary theory as well as 'origin of life' biology, quoted in The Case For A Creator, Lee Strobel, p78
7. Robin Collins, a physicist, mathematician, author and philosopher who studied under the legendary Alvin Platinga, quoted in The Case For A Creator, Lee Strobel, p132
8. Robin Collins
9. Roger Penrose in The Emperor's Mind, quoted in The Case for a Creator, p135
10. Guillermo Gonzalez, astronomer, physicist and co-author of Privileged Planet, quoted in The Case for a Creator, p174
11. Guillermo Gonzalez, quoted in The Case For A Creator, p169, 171
12. Lee Strobel, The Case For A Creator, pp157, 178

13. Robin Collins, quoted in The Case For A Creator, p131

14. Guillermo Gonzalez, quoted in The Case For A Creator, p185

15. Guillermo Gonzalez, Quoted in The Case For A Creator, p187

16. Jay Richards, philosopher and theologian, co-author of Privileged Planet, quoted in The Case For A Creator, p188

17. Jay Richards, quoted in The Case For A Creator, p189

18. See Creation's Tiny Mystery by Dr. Robert Gentry [or go to www.halos.com on the internet]

19. Ralph Muncaster, A Skeptic's Search For God, 2002, p93

20. Ralph Muncaster, A Skeptic's Search For God, 2002, p98

21. Ralph Muncaster, A Skeptic's Search For God, 2002, p93

22. Walter Bradley, PhD, professor at Texas A&M in The Mystery Of Life's Origin.

23. Discover, November, 2002

24. John Horgan, NewYork Times, Dec 25, 2002

25. Michael Behe, author of Darwin's Black Box, quoted in The Case For A Creator, p215

26. Cornelius Hunter in Darwin's God

27. George Wald, Scientific American, May 1954

28. Lee Strobel (as an atheist) in The Case For A Creator, p29

29. Freidrich Nietzche

30. Thomas Nagel, The Last Word, 1997, p130

31. Bill Bryson in A Short History Of Nearly Everything, pp 10 -13
32. National Geographic Encyclopedia Of Space, 2005, p.93
33. Bill Bryson in A Short History Of Nearly Everything
34. Quoted in Icons Of Evolution, Jonathan Wells, p221
35. Quoted in Icons Of Evolutiion, Jonathan Wells, p222
36. Jonathan Wells, Icons Of Evolution,2000, p228
37. Paul Davies in Nature
38. The Resurrection And The Life, 1911, p 24

CHAPTER II

TRUTH RELATIVISM PLURALISM

I was returning home from work in my van when I heard this question over the radio: "Is your religion true because you believe it OR do you believe your religion because it is true?" That question gripped me, and I could not get it off my mind. At first I was tempted to treat it like a party riddle that a slick answer would easily dismiss. But when I tried to answer the question, I realized how profound it really was. The more I thought about it, the more complex it appeared. I jotted down some ramifications to each side to help me clarify them. The first, I labeled as a belief-based religion and the other as truth [or evidence]-based.

If my religion was mainly belief-based, then:

[1] Every religion on earth would have to be accepted as true so long as somebody believed

it. For that matter, every statement, even if diametrically opposed to another would have to be acceptable.

[2] I could create the characteristics of 'God' by my belief. If I believed God to be very strong, only then would that be true. If I believed 'God' to be harsh and inconsiderate, well then He was just that kind of God.

[3] Belief would have the power to create truth.

[4] My faith would totter if I met an overwhelming problem, because I would know in the back of my mind that the 'God' I had created by my fancy was not bigger than the problem that I now faced in real life.

If my religion was evidence-based, then:

[1] Every religion/statement would not carry the same weight. I would have to study the merits and demerits of each and place them on different levels of credibility.

[2] 'God' would possess His own attributes whether I believed them or not. I could acknowledge them, but I could not bestow any on Him.

[3] Truth would create belief/faith [and not the other way round].

[4] I would have to provide sufficient evidence as a basis for my belief.

This led me to the all-important question – Could I honestly say that my religion was evidence-based; that I had good reason for my belief?

One day when I was alone at home, I thought it was time to address the question. I decided to play 'court of law' in my living room. I was going to be the judge, the jury, the defendant, the defense counsel and the prosecuting attorney. The oaths taken, the session began. Within ten minutes the jury, along with the public, was laughing and nearly taunting the defense counsel – so pathetic was the case and the arguments being presented! What began as a confident approach to establish my religion as very reasonable and well-based, crumbled before my face. Every further attempt only made it more ridiculous.

I was devastated!

When I had recovered from the shock, I decided to go on a journey of inquiry to settle this question for myself. I would keep at it till I returned with a satisfactory answer or realized there was none to be found.

TRUTH - RELATIVISM

Some say that truth is not knowable. It is out there but we cannot grasp it with sufficient certainty to feel comfortable about it. So, all a person can say is, "This is my truth and that is yours." Nobody can claim to know real truth.

Others are equally firm in their stand that truth is knowable. Absolute truth may be beyond us, but what we can know is objective enough to refer to as fact.

I had to grapple with these claims before continuing, because my journey would not be necessary if there was no chance of knowing the *truth* of the matter. What was this thing called 'truth' anyway?

There are multiple concepts and definitions; enough to make one reel. So, I narrowed them down to fit my quest for the reality of God. There are three basic ideas historically.

First, what is called Traditional Theism. The reference is to a sacred written code like the Quran or the Bhagavad Gita. Only the privileged few, the priestly class, may enter its holy precincts and then come out to us common people to instruct us on the meaning of the written text and the application of those mysterious pages to our lives.

Second, called Modernism [synonymous with scientific truth]. A few centuries old now, this challenged the exclusive rights of the clergy and established the scientific method of approach to truth. Anyone, not just the priestly class, could know truth, but it had to come only through the proper steps of investigation. Theories, experiments, data-collection and analysis of that data resulting in a conclusion, were the steps. The conclusions alone could be accepted as truth; all else was suspect.

Third, called Post-modernism [synonymous with subjectivism and relativism]. This rules the intellectual world of today. It dismissed the two earlier ones with a sweeping claim, "There is no such thing as truth. All statements are only relatively true and therefore relatively false. Nobody can claim to establish a fact anywhere in the world."

Phew! If there ever was a pot-pouri of ideas!

I decided to examine them all.

Traditional Theism. Looking down history, the first impression was one of disgust and horror. The inhumanly cruel crusades, the murderous, mind-jarring jihads, the perfidious papal inquisitions were all repulsive. If this was what those writings about God instigated, I did not want it at all. I turned away in revulsion.

Modernism. The method appealed to me. It was open and objective. The attempt to be precise was impressive, the mathematical calculations often going to the fourth and fifth decimal places. But the big drawback was the complete absence of the search for God. In fact the idea of the supernatural was ridiculed. The focus was elsewhere and I could not see any likely change in the near future. I would have to leave it to another generation perhaps.

Relativism. This appeared broad and easy-going. You have your truth; I have mine. I scratch your back; you mine. But that was until the question of absolute truth came up. Then it was a bitter fight with no quarters given and no compromise possible. Even the definition of absolute truth pertaining only to our sphere of existence was not acceptable. [One such definition: Absolute truth is that which is valid for all people, at all times, at all places.] See page 197, **Appendix II,** for my examination of this concept. It was not even a philosophy. A mere 'mood', as Ravi Zacharias labeled it, it did not stand up to scrutiny.

At this point I was in an awful intellectual bind. I had discarded all three concepts. But I would still have to make decisions throughout the day. What principles would govern those decisions? A basis was needed at every step. A vacuum was just not possible. I realized I had somehow reached a false conclusion. I would have to re-think this through.

To my great relief I found a discrepancy that left a door of inquiry still open. In examining modernism and post-modernism I had grappled with the substance of what they were claiming. I had tried to weigh the arguments for and against the claims. But with traditional theism I had slid off that point and had focused on the nasty behavior of certain people. These I had equated with the stuff; the substance of their claims. I was right in my evaluation of the behavior; but wrong in connecting it to the written claims. Sure, bad behavior was present, but that was not all there was to it. I had met some exceptional, wonderful people too. They were generous, pleasant, purposeful and selfless and I had a deep sense of admiration for them. They had clearly been a blessing to the community in which they lived. When asked for the secret, they pointed to their religious beliefs. So, here was traditional truth producing both torture as well as tremendous good. We all know families in which one child grows to become accomplished and graceful while another turns out the scum of society. How fair would it be to point to only the scumbag and discredit the family? No, it would not be fair to focus on just one side and ignore the other. I decided to check out the *substance* of traditional truth [traditional theism].

PLURALISM

I was not prepared for what I next faced. Even a cursory glance left me stunned. From the scanty claims of the Sumerians, the Mayans, the Egyptians and the legendary writings of the ancient Chinese and the Indians, to the more structured writings of Zarathustra [Zoroaster], Gautama Buddha, The Hindu Veda's, the Analects of Confucius, Lao Tzu's Taoism, the Old and New Testaments of the Bible, the Talmud, the Quran, it was a bewildering array that left me shaken. Dismayed and despairing I sat down to think again. I had hit a stone wall. Multiple life-times would not be enough to study them all. Painstakingly I had come this far. Would it be finally futile?

Cautiously I began to ask around. What did others think of this daunting spectrum? Gradually, two opposing camps came into view.

Camp one [Exclusivism], in which, each boldly claimed that there was only one correct way – "Mine"!

Camp two [Pluralism], which said that all the religions were only different paths to the same, final destination.

Both camps could not be correct.

I decided to look at Pluralism first. If that could be established, I need not be alarmed because I was already on a safe path. My search would be to only get more information within my own belief system. I could spare myself the struggle of delving into a hazy, nebulous field looking for something that I did not even know existed. See page 207, Appendix III, for the scrutiny.

It did not stand up to my examination. The obstacles were insurmountable and I had to discard it. The claims were different paths and were definitely aimed at different destinations.

I turned my attention to Exclusivism. I had rejected Pluralism with good reason, but was by no means out of the woods yet, for here were multiple claims, each clamoring for the status of 'The Only Way'.

What were the options I would need to consider? There were three.

First, ALL are correct. This is absurd and illogical. It would be like saying there are multiple Prime Ministers in India or multiple Presidents in the US. This was not a real option.

Second, ALL are wrong. This was not illogical; it did not go against reason. But there were two obstacles I could not get around.

1. To say that anything was wrong was to imply that I knew what was right and could use that special knowledge as a yardstick. But nobody

on earth has the position, the knowledge or authority to make such a claim. I could not.

2. If all were wrong, I would have to discard them all because they had lied at a fundamental level leaving me no assurance regarding anything else uttered. Also, one core claim found among the religions was the existence of the supernatural. I would have to discard that concept too. But I had already established it to a reasonable degree at the start of my search. I could not say they *all* were wrong.

Third, the only one left – Somewhere out there, there was one claim and ONLY ONE that was legitimate! Only one that was truly the ONLY WAY. In other words there was ONLY ONE WAY to truth. Even if I would never be able to identify it, the credibility of this statement would stand.

As it sunk in, I realized that it was a critical, pivotal point of my search. Everything that followed would have to be held to this concept. It would become the uncompromising reference point henceforth. It was very frightening too. What if I was not on that path? What if I failed to recognize it?

I pondered over the significance of this crucial conclusion.

1. The conclusion was reached by a step-wise deduction from a 'neutral' angle and therefore was credible.
2. It refuted the concept of Pluralism.

3. It did not allow the followers of these religions to toy around with Pluralism. For example, if a Muslim espoused pluralism, he would have to first deny the claims of Allah and the Islamic faith itself.

4. The 'Only Way' claim was a fundamental one. If a religion could not establish itself as the 'Only Way', it would lose its standing because it had lied at a basic level. It would have relevance only at the points in which it agreed with the 'Only Way'.

5. It was the most powerful motivating statement that could be made. It was meant to beckon one and all to that particular fold. Each founder wanted the followers to take him seriously; forsake every other path and stay loyal no matter what the cost.

6. The distance between the top and the rest did not matter. Winning by even the slimmest of margins, would be enough. A thousandth of a second can separate the Olympic champion from every other contender and relegate them to the 'also-ran' status.

7. A more critical factor than being ahead was being different. If there were four red marbles and only one that was green, then the green would be the one. If all but one were traveling west, then east would be the right direction. If all were running and only one was walking, then walking was the correct way to compete.

Whatever the significance, the question now was, how to do the comparison. What method would I use to compare apples and oranges? It was not possible to just describe the different features and make a choice based on my likes and dislikes. That would not help because each of us has our own set of likes and dislikes. However there was one possible way out of this predicament. If the apple was ripe, sweet and fresh while the orange was old, rotten and full of worms, the choice would not be difficult to make, especially when hungry. Notice, however that the comparison was not actually between the apple and the orange but between 'freshness' and 'rottenness'. Yet it would be a very reasonable choice that nobody would seriously disagree with. Once freshness was preferred, the apple became the automatic choice.

Similarly I knew I could not directly compare the different tenets of beliefs and the various doctrines to decide which was superior. I had no set of criteria that was universally accepted as a reference point to which I could bring the religious features for a stan-dardized study. I would have to find other features that would indirectly help me make a choice.

What follows are the results of using those features. I initially chose five of the world's great religions and made a comparison asking ten questions of each of them and looking for responses from their writings or from sources friendly to them — Hinduism, Islam, Christianity, Judaism and Buddhism. Three questions were to be addressed to the writings and seven to the flesh-and-blood founders of each religion. I would try not to discredit or down-play any claim. I would simply lay them side by side and score them as fairly as possible.

The questions were such that anyone could look for the answers. It did not require a specific religious interpretation. I was looking for the *facts* on which the adherents had made their religious interpretations. The part relating to the interpretation is religious and constitutes the claims of that religion. The part relating to the 'facts', however, is not religious by nature. I did not have to be a follower to accept it. It is to this point I directed my questions.

The ten questions:

1. What type of literature is the writing?
2. Does the writing open itself to be challenged for authenticity?
3. What is a top feature of the writing?
4. What is the highest claim of the founder for himself?
5. What is the nature of the message/mission of the founder?
6. How does the life of the founder compare with his own teaching?
7. How does the length of ministry compare with the results?
8. What are the reports of the birth of the founder?
9. What were the circumstances at death of the founder?
10. What was the post-death scene?

I wondered if anything decisive would come out of such a process. Yes, the evaluations were going to be subjective. I was free to give whatever score I thought best. Nobody was looking over my shoulders to see if I was playing it fair. But if I was not honest, I would be fooling only myself. To me, this was serious business and too much was at stake to try to manipulate the outcome.

Of course questions will remain. They may make my decisions look bad. But a bad decision could be a good one – if the alternative is worse! [Conversely, a good decision could be bad if there was a better option.]

So, keep your seat belts fastened with humility, honesty, calmness and respect. The landscape ahead looks exciting. It is going to be quite a journey!

CHAPTER III

LITERATURE

The Principle of Verifiability suggests that if there were two conflicting claims which could not be assessed directly, but they did have indirect factors which could be evaluated, then the one that was attached to a verifiable factor gained in credibility.

For example:

The location of dim stars has sometimes been predicted, even before being visualized. This is done by observing the movements of nearby visible stars, resulting from the gravitational pull between the celestial bodies. Later, with better telescopes and viewing techniques, the star would come into actual view. Now, suppose Astronomer A predicted the location of a star to be below the belt of the constellation Orion, while Astronomer B said it was above the belt. Both agreed that it was not visible to the naked eye. Astronomer A offered no information other than his 'gut' feelings which had served him well earlier, while Astronomer B produced the results of prolonged studies showing the movements of nearby stars. This information had been double-checked by others and found to be reliable. This verifiable portion made the claim of B more credible. The star was most probably above the belt.

Similarly, the concepts of truth and doctrines in the ancient sacred writings cannot be tested directly for value and authenticity. But they have been handed down to us in the context of narratives which can be tested for their historical reliability. The point of contact between the supernatural [religious claims] and humans has to be in the mundane world first – in the course of day-to-day human existence. Secular history is the fundamental record of that existence. Therefore, religious claims should have a historical context, to have merit. The more concrete the historical terms like events, places and dates, the more the likelihood of the attached abstract claims, like the nature of God and truth, being the original, authentic message.

There are four broad categories that the ancient writings may be classified into.

A. **Folk Tales:** There is no attempt to state a real/true story. In fact, it is accepted that the narrative is fictional. The main intent is to be interesting and bring out a lesson/moral.

B. Legend: This is probably based on a true story, but changes crept in over a period – exaggerations and embellishments to super-human proportions. These are slipped in generations after the event, when there are no longer any eye-witnesses to challenge the change. The time period required is usually centuries.

C. Myth: They are so far back in history that imagination is accepted as the main ingre-dient. The characters and stories are most probably not true. The bizarre and unnatural elements are emphasized in as colorful a description as possible. The time period is usually many centuries, and even millennia.

D. Historical: The attempt is to state the story as it really was. There are no significant addi-tions and no core changes due to distortions or overstatements. The closer the formation and recording of the narrative to the time of the event, the greater the credibility.

Let us see how the writings fare.

I. **Hinduism:** The earliest wrings are the Veda's; followed by the anthology, the Upanishads; then the Ramayana Epic and lastly the Mahabharata Epic within which is found the Bhagavad-gita.

"Lord Krishna first spoke Bhagavad-gita to the Sun-god some 100's of millions of years ago"[1]

It was lost and then repeated at the Battle of Kurukshetra about 50 centuries ago. Such a distant past makes it impossible to check the stories out. Most scholars accept the mythological nature of the writings.

II. **Buddhism:** The next four statements, in chronological order, regarding Gautama Buddha are from Buddhism The Light Of Asia by K. K. S Chen, pp 62 – 64

   a. "Was he not born at Lumbini? ... Did he not complete existence at Kusinara?" "... the Theravada looked upon the master as a human teacher"

   b. "Soon after the passing of the master a change began to set in."

   c. "At the beginning of the Christian era, the transcendental nature of the Buddha became more and more pronounced."

   d. "In one of the most important pieces of Mahayana literature there is not much of the man left in the Buddha. He is now an exalted being who has lived for countless ages in the past and will continue to live forever."

This covers a period of about one thousand years in which there is a clear change regarding the nature of the Buddha from an ordinary human to a super-human level.

III. **Judaism:** There are thirty-nine different books and over twenty authors living at vastly different periods of history. I could not find a way to give one consistent classification to the whole set of writings.

IV. **Islam:** The Quran was put together in writing by 652 CE – within thirty years of the life of Muhammad. The earliest manuscripts were destroyed by one of the Caliphs, such that only one version remained. So, we cannot compare what we have today with what there was in the beginning. However, since the first one was within one generation, we should place it among the historical type of literature.

V. **Christianity:** The earliest written documents were the letters of Paul, some of which were written within ten years of the life of Jesus. He came into the movement later compared to the disciples of Jesus, and so the information was established orally even before that. There appears to have been no gap between the formation of the story and the events from which it was culled. The Gospels themselves, though of later date, were all written in the life-time of that generation. "We can already say emphatically that there is no longer any solid basis for dating any book of the New Testament after about AD 80." Sir William Albright, one of the greatest archeologists in the world.[2]

The New Testament should be classified as a historical piece of literature.

That does not mean it cannot be questioned. It only means it cannot be treated as a legendary or mythological story. It means that the questions have to be dealt with in terms of historical evidence – much like we would debate the circumstances around the death of the late President JF Kennedy in Dallas in 1963. Nobody takes JFK to be a mythological figure and doubts the crux of his biography just because of those questions, not to mention the severe differences in the 'authoritative' reports making the rounds even today.

How does the New Testament compare with other ancient classics which are accepted as unquestionably historical the world over?

Cesar's Gallic Wars was written in 100 BC. The earliest copy is dated 900 AD.

Herodotus' History, was written in 400 BC and earliest copy is dated 1300 AD.

Tacitus's Annals, was written in 100 AD and the earliest copy is dated 1100 AD.

Note the gaps – more than a thousand years! We have no idea whether what we have in our hands is really what the author wrote, and yet they are accepted without question by the general public. After swallowing a thousand years, it would not be fair to question and cavil over less than ten years.

Another pointer to whether or not the text is authentic is the number of manuscripts the literature is backed by. The smaller the number, the easier for changes to be made in all the copies. The greater the number, the more spread out geographically and time-wise, the more difficult to slip in the same changes in all the copies. The Gallic Wars is backed by ten manuscripts; Herodotus History by eight and Tacitus Annals by twenty. Homer's Iliad is high up there with an impressive six hundred and forty-three manuscripts. When it comes to the New Testament, it is far and away, not only the leader, but in a class by itself, with 5664 Greek manuscripts! If the Latin, Ethiopic, Slavic, Armenian etc are added, the total comes to an astounding 24,000 +![3]

> "In real terms the New Testament is easily the best attested ancient writing in terms of the sheer number of documents, the time span between the events and the document, and the variety of documents available to sustain or contradict it. There is nothing in ancient manuscript evidence to match such textual integrity..."[4]

> "No other ancient book has anything like such early and plentiful testimony to its text, and no unbiased scholar would deny that the text that has come down to us is substantially sound."[5]

> "In the variety and fullness of evidence on which it rests, the text of the New Testament stands absolutely and unapproachably alone among ancient prose writings."[6]

"To be skeptical of the resultant text of the New Testament books is to allow all of classical antiquity to slip into obscurity, for no documents of the ancient period are as well-attested bibliographically as the New Testament."[7]

I've heard numerous jokes and taunts regarding the 'miracles' in the Bible because it is treated as a myth. It is taken to be like the legends of yore, such as the Nordic Tales or the Arabian Nights, to be swallowed with a pinch of salt. I suppose, this is expected on just a superficial consideration; but when fairly and closely examined, the facts point to a different classification.

We should let the evidence speak for itself.

REFERENCES

1. Bhagavad-gita As It Is, Bhaktivedanta Book Trust, 1968, p xix
2. Recent Discoveries in Bible Lands, 1955, p136
3. See Josh McDowell, The New Evidence That Demands A Verdict, p34
4. Ravi Zacharias, Can Man Live Without God, 1994, p162
5. Sir Frederic Kenyon, The Bible and Modern Scholarship, 1948, p20
6. F.J.A. Hort, quoted in New Evidence That Demands A Verdict, Josh McDowell, p35
7. John W. Montgomery, History and Christianity, InterVarsity Press, p29

CHAPTER IV

CHALLENGE

Did the writings have any form of check-points? Was the inquirer free to check it out for himself? Was there a claim that could be examined for authenticity? Or, was testing and examination discouraged? Was I supposed to swallow the claims without question?

I. **Hinduism:** "... we have to accept it as it is; otherwise there is no point in trying to understand the Bhagavad-gita and its speaker, Lord Krishna."[1]

II. **Buddhism:** "... the genuine realization of the emptiness of the phenomenal world is ... a direct intuition of the highest truth. Absolute truth ... is unconditional undeterminate and beyond thought and word."[2]

In both these religions, the real-life experience of the follower was supposed to be the authenticating feature. It appeared a good, bold point which made a lot of sense. However, if there were many religions out there, how practical would it be to get into the experience of each before making a decision? Indeed, to get into the experience of any particular one required a choice. Added to that were the clear warnings from the different religions, of awful consequences of going into any other path than what it had outlined. Experience before choice, to me, was putting the cart before the horse. I wanted a reason that I could think through before I checked it out by experience.

III. **Islam:** "If men and jinn combined to produce a book akin to this Quran, they would surely fail to produce its like, though they helped one another as best they could."[3] In other places the challenge is to produce ten chapters like the Quran (11:13), or even one chapter (10:38).

Here is a stated challenge. But when I attempted to test it out, there were four snags that killed the attempt.

a. The challenge did not state what feature was to be equaled – whether it was the prose or poetry or rhythm or diction or philosophy or doctrine or beliefs or descriptions of God etc.

b. It did not define the method of comparison. How would a decision be made whether the Quran was better, equal or worse?

c. Who would be the final judge regarding the comparison? Would it be an Imam, a Muslim Council, a neutral body, an international committee or an individual like me? By default, I felt that I should be the judge. If so, then I think there are other writings that can equal the Quran in one or more aspects – Omar Khayyam, Rabindranath Tagore, Jallaluddin Rumi, to name a few. To me, these writings are too beautiful to be surpassed.

d. The Language. To the orthodox Muslim, Arabic is the divine language of communication and the Quran is considered authentic only in that language. Hence to equal the Quran, the writing should be only in the Arabic language. I'm sure there are millions of Muslims who do not know one sentence of literary Arabic. What then of the rest of the world? I was definitely not included in this challenge. The test had lost its universal character.

A subjective, nebulous challenge, applicable to only a narrow segment of the world's population is not a real challenge.

IV. **Judeo-Christian:** "'Present your case', says the Lord ... ' Let them bring forth and show us what will happen ... declare to us things to come. Show the things that are to come hereafter, that we may know that you are gods.'".[4] This challenge is called predictive prophecy, meaning that both the prediction and the actual occurrence could be verified and established as separate entities. It is an intriguing test because it involves 'time'. We humans are totally unable to break through the barriers of time except in imagination. We can guess what might happen later, depending on certain trends, but we cannot predict with certainty anything say, a century or even a decade, before it happens. The test points to super-human knowledge.

Here is an example of such a prophecy: The Bible in Jeremiah 51:36,37 stated, "I will make her springs dry ... Babylon shall become a heap ... without an inhabitant." At the time of this prediction, said to be about 595 BCE, Babylon was at its zenith. The walls – fully fortified, broad enough for two chariots to run side by side and rising to heights of 200 feet – were considered impregnable. The food supplies in the stores were sufficient to last for twenty years, making mockery of anyone planning a siege. But it fell to Cyrus the Medo-persian in one day. He conquered it by draining the river Euphrates which ran under and across the city, into aqueducts that his soldiers dug, then marching his army into the city on the riverbed, once the 'springs were dry'. And today, "Few words evoke as many images of ancient decadence, glory and prophetic doom as does 'Babylon'.

Yet the actual place, 50 miles south of Baghdad – is flat, hot, *deserted*, dusty."[5]

It is still 'without an inhabitant'. You and I are witnesses to the fulfillment of this prophecy.

If I predicted that your son would have curly black hair, when everyone in the family had straight blond hair; at the age of four he would read all the works of Shakespeare; at twelve he would graduate from university with a professional degree; at twenty he would win an Olympic gold medal in swimming; at thirty he would be awarded the Nobel prize in Astrophysics, and if they all came true, I dare say, you would follow me to the ends of the earth to find out what my next prediction was going to be. Of course you would! It would be an astounding set of predictions setting me apart as 'out of this world'. How many more true predictions would be needed to establish my credentials? I would be satisfied with a dozen, wouldn't you?

Scholars tell us that there are *six hundred* predictions in the Old and New Testaments of the Bible which have come to pass. Over three hundred pertain to one individual, Jesus the Christ. Over two dozen were fulfilled during one week-end and some of them were predicted more than *one thousand years* before the events.[6]

The Judeo-Christian challenge is open and clear, and can be checked out by any ordinary person willing to do it and be honest about it.

REFERENCES

1. Bhagavad-gita As It Is, Preface, p xix
2. KKS Chen, Buddhism, The Light Of Asia, 1968, p76
3. Quran 17:88
4. Old Testament, Isaiah 41: 22, 23
5. Smithsonian, June 2003, p50 [emphasis mine]
6. See Josh McDowell's The New Evidence That Demands A Verdict and Ralph Muncaster's A Skeptic's Search For God

CHAPTER V

TOP FEATURE

These religions have more than one great feature. I picked some out at random and yet, these are considered the top ones by many. They are all very, very impressive.

I. **Islam:** The language of the Quran is often spoken about and praised to the skies. "When they listen to it, they feel enveloped in a Divine dimension of sound." Tradition has it that in 616 CE there was a certain Umar ibn Al- Khattab who was angry with the new religion, and went looking for Muhammad to kill him. He was deflected from his purpose and sent back home where, to his consternation, he found that the hated Quran was being read right under his own roof. He punched his sister in the face and everyone fled, leaving the Quran on the ground. He picked it up and read the opening verses of chapter

20 and, "'How fine and noble is this speech', he said wonderingly, and this Muslim was felled ... by the beauty of the Quran which reached through his passionate hatred and prejudice to an inner receptivity that he had not been aware of." He now went looking for Muhammad to confess his instant conversion to the new religion.[1]

There are other stories of ordinary people as well as kings and rulers who were struck with the beauty of the language and accepted the religion and friendship of the Muslims to the point of becoming staunch military allies.

"In the Quran, Muhammad is often called the ' Ummi' prophet, the unlettered prophet." [Karen Armstrong, p88]. Muhammad could not read or write. Others wrote it out for him or memorized what he was saying and kept the information bank growing. That is why the book is called the Quran which means 'The Recitation'. Muslims claim this to be a great miracle and an attestation of its super-human origin.

The language of the Quran is amazing, exquisitely beautiful and possibly super-natural.

II. **Hinduism:** "Hindu sages gave to mankind one of the most sophisticated systems of philosophy ever devised."[2]

Taken together, the Veda's, the Upanishads, the Epics and other traditional writings, form a grand network of information. They contain a blend of religion, ethics, civil codes, medicine, mathematics, astronomy and other natural sciences thousands of years old and yet, which astonish us today, in the twenty-first century.

They, arguably, invented the concept of 'zero' which can represent nothing, as well as the largest number imaginable. Without the decimal system, maths and science would come to a standstill.

The Ayurvedic system of medicine has ideas that Allopathy has not understood yet.

There are divisions of time (called 'kashta') going down to the hundred millionth of a second. The only point where science uses such numbers is in describing the half-lives of sub-atomic radio-isotopes like the mesons and baryons, which we have come to know about only recently.

Hindu Philosophy and information is also amazing, deep and brilliant, and possibly super-natural.

III. **Buddhism:** The literature is vast, detailed and mysterious.

    a. Vastness: "The 'Pali' cannon fills 45 huge volumes ... the Chinese scriptures consist of 100 volumes of 1000 closely printed pages each, while the Tibetan extends to 325 volumes."[3] That's a total of four hundred and seventy thousand pages!

Half of which is yet to be translated from the original languages.

b. Detail: "The Lord's body had thirty-two marks of a super-man, and was adorned with the eighty subsidiary characteristics. He was endowed with the eighteen special dharmas of a Buddha, mighty with the ten powers of a tathagata and in possession of the four grounds of self-confidence."[4]

The monks were subject to 250 rules if you were male and to 311 rules if you were female.

A common prayer for forgiveness went, "I beg leave, I beg leave, I beg leave. May I be freed at all times from the four states of woe, the three scourges, the eight wrong circumstances, the five enemies, the four deficiencies, the five misfortunes and quickly attain the path ..."[5]

c. Mystery: "The bulk of this literature is couched in a deliberately mysterious language which would convey nothing to the average reader." For Example, "The realization that undifferentiated emptiness is the sole absolute truth. Nirvana is therefore that mental state in which one realizes that all things are really non-existent."[6]

Buddhist Scriptures are also amazing, awesome and mysterious and possibly super-natural.

IV. Judeo-Christian: The Cross-references among the authors is unique.

For example, between the authors of the Old Testament: "I, Daniel, understood by the books, the number of the years specified by the word of the Lord through Jeremiah the prophet ..."[7] Daniel is recommending Jeremiah.

Between authors of the New Testament: "... as also our beloved brother Paul, according to the wisdom given him, has written to you ..."[8] Peter is upholding Paul.

Between authors of the Old and New Testaments: "So, all this was done that it might be fulfilled which was spoken by the Lord through the prophet Isaiah saying ..."[9] Matthew is endorsing Isaiah.

Each was confessing that the 'source' of their own information, [the Lord], was also the 'source' of the previous authors even if it was many hundreds of years earlier. This 'source' then supervised the writing of the whole Bible and therefore had to live for at least 1400 years! That is not within the realm of human achievement.

The writing of the Judeo-Christian Scripture is also amazing, and beyond human capability — 'super-natural'.

They all are awe-inspiring and have the qualities to even dazzle an honest inquirer. This is one reason why it is difficult for me to give weight to the pluralist who wants to treat all these features as if they were mundane enough to be impugned. What are the characteristics and credentials he can produce for himself, that would be impressive enough for me to accept *his* pronouncements on a par with those having such marks of distinction? Each religion has a brilliance its own and each has the right to stake its claim to being the only way. To simply lump them together as a homogenized mixture is not doing justice to the outstanding features they portray. It is the honest response to say "WOW!" to each feature described in this chapter.

And now let us turn to the founders.

REFERENCES

1. Karen Armstrong, Muhammad,1992, p128
2. National Geographic, Atlas of the World, 1975, p119
3. Buddhist Scriptures, Edward Conze, Penguin Books, 1959, p41
4. Buddhist Scriptures, Edward Conze, Penguin Books, 1959, p22
5. Jesus Among Other Gods, Ravi Zacharias, 2000, p90
6. KKS Chen, Buddhism, The Light Of Asia, 1968, p72
7. Old Testament, Daniel 9:2
8. New Testament, II Peter 3:15
9. New Testament, Matthew 1:22

CHAPTER VI

HIGHEST CLAIM

We often think of claims as inferior to fact; a little hollow and lacking in substance. But we rely on them very heavily when making decisions. I just bought a laptop computer looking at the printed slip which described the features. I really had no idea whether the hard drive possessed the capacity or the speed of the system the slip claimed. Yet I paid the price and brought it home. We do this numerous times a day in various situations. Bold claims, especially written ones, give us some assurance that what they are saying is true.

I decided to compare the highest claim that the flesh-and-blood founders made for themselves. I was going to take them at face-value without questioning their veracity because, just like in the case of my computer, I had no way of either confirming or refuting them.

I.   Hinduism: There is no single founder, but a host of authors. The highest claim of the authors was that of a sage— one who is respected and revered for his knowledge, integrity, piety and exceptional insight into spiritual matters.

II. Islam: Muhammad was called the 'Seal of the Prophets'. Islamic tradition tells us that Allah sent down 124,000 prophets beginning from Adam; but Muhammad was the final one whose words could not be challenged.

III. Buddhism: Gautama Buddha claimed to be the super-enlightened one. After a search for six years, he was enlightened, in stages during one night, while under a ficus tree in Bodh Gaya, India.

IV. Judaism: Moses was the acclaimed prophet of Jehovah and the Law-giver in Israel.

V.   Christianity: Jesus claimed to be the Son of God.

Even a cursory glance revealed that while every claim was great and awesome, the claim of Jesus was 'out of this world', literally. All the others were in the human realm; his was in the realm of 'God'. The others claimed to have some contact with that dimension; Jesus claimed to belong to that dimension. The difference was too stark to miss. When the people of his day heard it, they exclaimed, "Is this not the carpenter's son? Don't we know his siblings?" The first response was of disbelief. Our first instinct is to dismiss it as a figure of speech or some other nonliteral expression. But the more I looked at it in the writings the clearer it became that that was exactly what he was claiming to be – God! But whoever heard of an ordinary peasant claiming to be God? Would it be worth the time to even try to disprove it?

And yet I realized one thing — this was the highest claim anyone could possibly make. No other founder had made it. If I was looking for some difference between the various claims, then here was a clear-cut one. And however unbelievable it sounded, it was written in the best attested piece of ancient literature. It was truly enigmatic – I realized how unbelievable it would sound to a rational thinker and yet it was not found in a mythological story. There was no way I could accept it wholeheartedly or spew it out without proper reason. Claiming to be an inquirer, I had no option but to treat it with respect, not disdain, and check it out calmly.

Frivolity aside, what kind of people would think of making such an outrageous claim?

There are four kinds:

1. Lunatics
2. Liars/imposters
3. Megalomaniacs and
4. God

Did Jesus fit in with any kind?

1. Lunatic: Was he crazy — deluded with visions of grandeur — imagining himself to be far above what he really was? The word- pictures

of deluded individuals are usually disjointed thoughts and absurd scenes that keep flitting from one to another, in which they are always riding the crest of the wave. But the sayings of Jesus did not have these qualities. I had not found a single scholar seriously charge him with insanity.

On the contrary there were many who were in awe of his deep and sublime teachings.

"Everything in Christ astonishes me ... the nearer I approach, the more carefully I examine, everything is above me – everything remains grand, of a grandeur which overpowers ... Neither history, nor humanity, nor the ages, nor nature offer me anything with which I am able to compare or explain it. Here everything is extraordinary."[1]

Regarding the words of Jesus, "They are read more, quoted more, loved more, believed more, and translated more because they are the greatest words ever spoken. And where is their greatness? Their greatness lies in the pure lucid spirituality in dealing clearly, definitively and authoritatively with the greatest problems that throb in the human breast."[2]

No, it would not be fair to label him 'mad'.

2. Liar/Imposter. All of his teachings had an undergirding of ethics and morals that won the admiration of some of his harshest critics. To accuse him of consistently lying at a fundamental point would go against the grain of his entire life and message. Transparent honesty and truthfulness were the major themes of his life.

   Yet one must concede that anybody can resort to falsehood at critical moments. None of us has been spared that temptation. But it is precisely at just such a moment that we find a pointer to the extent of his commitment to what he believed. The scene is the trial before the Sanhedrin. One final question would wrap up the proceedings. Placing Jesus under the ultimate oath to a Jewish ear, the Chief Priest asks, "Tell us, are you the Son of God?" He knew only too well the consequences. To answer in the affirmative would bring upon himself the instant charge of blasphemy and the punishment of death – exactly what these guardians of the law had been scheming for and desperately working towards for a long time.

   People go to great lengths to produce truthful evidence to escape the death sentence. Others have been known to fall back to any form of pretense and falsehood to avoid the death sentence. But no one in his right mind has been known to cling to falsehood and lie under oath to hang himself. Jesus answered in the affirmative and brought upon himself the death sentence. There can be no higher evidence for the truthfulness of this man. He was not crazy, nor was he a liar. He had to believe, from the depths of his heart, that he was the Son of God.

3. Megalomaniac. The Pharaohs of Egypt and the Emperors of Rome were examples of those who demanded worship as gods on pain of severe punishment and even death. These they did not hesitate to mete out because they had absolute power, including military power, in their hands. What was this man's position and military power? He had none. Did he constantly make demands for self-aggran- dizements? Consider his words, "I came to serve and not to be served." "... to minister and not to be ministered unto."[3]

In the east, even today, there is a custom of washing the feet of a guest who has come home. Usually it is the one lowest in the social ladder on whom the task falls. There was a time when Jesus and his disciples arrived at a home and there was no servant to wash their feet. Each looked at the other wondering who would stoop to this lowliest of jobs. Silently this man rose up, took off his outer garments, wrapped himself with a towel and taking a basin of water, washed the dirty feet of his disciples. No megalomaniac has ever been known to bow himself before his followers in such humility. Then he turned to his disciples and admonished them to wash one another's feet. Teaching and example dove-tailed into a portrait, not of a bloated ego, but of self-abnegation. This is not the picture of one drunk with power.

4. God. Really and truly God. This is the only option now left. But it is not easy to swallow. Could it be true that this 'next door neighbor' belongs to the realm of God? He appears too ordinary, and belief struggles to accept the claim. But the question persists, however weakly or strongly, "Could it be true?"

Some try a compromise. He was not a deceiver; he was just honestly mistaken. "A fourth possibility, almost too obvious to need mentioning, is that Jesus was honestly mistaken. Plenty of people are."[4] This is a totally unrealistic explanation. One can be honestly mistaken about where the pen was left or regarding a face in a crowd; but not regarding being the Queen of England or having just landed on Mars! Honestly mistaken about being God? That is being ludicrous.

Others want to give the maximum that common sense will allow: He was a good and great man, a prophet and moral teacher, but not God. But his claim was unequivocal, that of being God. Like someone said, "If he is not God, he is not good."

"I am trying here to prevent anyone saying the really foolish thing that people often say about Him: ' I'm ready to accept Jesus as a great moral teacher, but I don't accept His claim to be God.' That is the one thing we must not say. A man who was merely a man and said the sort of things Jesus said would not be a great moral teacher. He would either be a lunatic – on a level with the man who says he is a poached egg – or else he would be the Devil of Hell. You must make your choice. Either this man was, and is, the Son of God: or else a mad man or something worse. You can shut Him up for a fool, you can spit at Him and kill Him as a demon; or you can fall at His feet and call Him Lord and God. But let us not come up with any patronizing nonsense about His being a great human teacher. He has not left that open to us. He did not intend to."[5]

Whether we accept the claim to be true or not, it has to be conceded that Jesus made the highest claim compared to any other founder. And because he did not fit easily and smoothly into the categories of ordinary humans known to have claimed a super-natural status, I could not dismiss his claim.

REFERENCES

1. Napoleon Bonaparte, quoted in The New Evidence That Demands a Verdict, Josh McDowell, p161
2. Bernard Ramm, Protestant Christian Evidences, Moody Press, pp170&171
3. New Testament, Matthew 20:28
4. Richard Dawkins, The God Delusion, 2006, p92
5. CS Lewis, Mere Christianity, 1952, p 40, 41

CHAPTER VII

MESSAGE & MISSION

Each founder had a unique story and a specific message to give. Each had a claim as to how the message came and why there was need for that message. This topic was too cumbersome to go into much detail. So, I decided to put the idea from each founder in a nutshell, in a sentence or two and then lay them side by side for a comparison.

    I. **Hinduism:** The sages and authors formed a philosophy to show the way to ultimate truth which is the merging of the human atma [spirit] into the Super Soul or Brahman, to break the cycle of life and death.

    II. **Buddhism:** "For enlightenment I was born, for the good of all that lives."[1] Gautama Buddha. He wanted to pass on the 'light' which was ultimate truth, which was ultimate 'nothingness'.

III. Islam: "For Muslims it (The Quran) is the infallible word of God ... revealed to the Prophet Muhammad by the Angel Gabriel."[2] The intent was to grasp and spread the word of God to the world.

IV. Judaism: "You shall therefore keep My statutes and My judgments, which if a man does, he shall live ..."[3] The key was to establish a set of the correct rules, treat it as a law and obey it implicitly to gain life.

V. Christianity: "I am the way, the truth and the life."[4] "I am the light of the world."[5] "I am the resurrection and the life."[6]

The words, "I Am" are unique. They are not found in the claims of any other founder. Every other founder could mark out the path, point to the method or way, and insist on showing and expounding the truth which was given to him. This man claimed to *be* the truth. He was not just bringing a message, he *was* the message. Nobody else ever claimed to be identical with the message they were bringing. In all the religions, it was the rules, regulations and precepts that were taught. Here it was a *person* who was being introduced; the person who claimed to have established the rules himself. It is the difference between reading a manual to fix a super-computer and having the master designer himself ready to consult and guide.

Every other founder claimed to have some contact with the 'other world' from where they got their light, truth and realizations. Buddha had to search for enlightenment. This was a confession that light was not inherent in him. Muhammad was revealed the Word by the Angel Gabriel. This was a confession that if there was no revelation, he would have had nothing to say. Moses clearly stated that all that he ever passed on to the Israelite nation was what he had received from Jehovah. He had nothing of himself to give.

If you take away the person of Muhammad, Islam and Allah will still remain.

If you take away the person of Buddha, Buddhism still remains.

If you take away Moses, Judaism remains.

If you take away Valmiki and Vyas, Hinduism remains.

If you take away Jesus, There is nothing left in Christianity.

It was not just a different claim he was making, although the difference is stark; it was also the position from which he was making the claim that was different, radically different.

Let me illustrate it with two comparisons.

First, with Gautama Buddha. Till the age of twenty-nine he was not enlightened at all. The next six years were spent in a relentless, desperate search. He tried various methods and ways. "To such a pitch of asceticism have I gone that naked was I, flouting life's decencies ... I have visited only one house a day and there taken only one morsel ... or one every seven days, or only once a fortnight ... I have plucked out the hair of my head and the hair of my beard ... having couched on thorns ... in diverse fashions, I have lived to torment and to torture my body, to such a length of asceticism have I gone."[7]

Finally after this rigorous penance, he attained enlightened one night, going through four successive stages of realizations. Even after that, he was not sure what to do with that 'light', and had to be coaxed by 'Brahma' to go ahead and deliver the message. In short, it was an all-consuming struggle to reach a goal. Let us grant that he did reach it. Compare this search and uncertainty with the story of Jesus.

Jesus did not need to struggle. There is no record of any desperate, torturous search for truth and light. He was never in a quandary regarding his claims. He simply said, "I am the light." He did not strain every nerve to reach the goal of truth; *he was the goal*. And from that vantage position he claimed to describe truth.

Second, with Muhammad. One of the most spiritual experiences described in his life was the Night Journey. This is cited as a powerful claim to his status as the 'Seal of the Prophets'. In the year 620, he was taken one night from Mecca on the heavenly steed Buruq to the Temple mount in Jerusalem. There a ladder was set up on which he and Gabriel climbed up through the seven heavens to the level of the throne of Allah. He returned to earth the same night. He was thus given an exalted privilege of having been in proximity to the Essence of Allah. Although there is some controversy whether this was a physical or mystical journey, let us grant that he did have this incredible experience.[8]

Inherent in this description is the confession that Muhammad belonged to this earth and he was allowed to travel up to heaven as a visitor for a brief glance at that wondrous place.

Contrast this with the claims of Jesus. Heaven, that wondrous place, was his dwelling place. He belonged there and had to come down to earth as a visitor for a specific purpose. *The origins and directions of travel between the two stand in exact reverse.*

Who would know more about New York and the nuances of the hectic life amidst the jostling crowds of Manhattan? One who has lived there all his life? Or one who flew in from India, took a guided tour of the city for a few hours and hopped onto the next flight heading home?

If we accept the claim that Buddha was enlightened and that Muhammad had the Night Journey, it would only be fair to accept the claim that Jesus came down from heaven, bringing the message in himself and could therefore say, "I Am". The claim clearly sets him apart from the others.

REFERENCES

1. Buddhist Scriptures, Edward Conze, Penguin Books, 1959, p36
2. Translation of the Quran by NJ Dawood, Introduction, p ix
3. Old Testament, Leviticus 18:5
4. New Testament, John 14:6
5. New Testament, John 8:12
6. New Testament, John 11:25
7. KKS Chen, Buddhism, The Light Of Asia, 1968, p 21.
8. Muhammad, Karen Armstrong, 1992, p138,139

CHAPTER VIII

TEACHING VERSUS LIFE

"By precept and example."
"By word and deed."
"Actions speak louder than words."
"What you are doing is so loud that I cannot hear what you are saying."

Consistency in the life of an individual — that's what makes the greater impact than any profession of the lips. The teachings the founders brought were all wonderful and deep; but what I wanted to know was whether their own life-actions had been brought into line with those teachings. This, to me, was the *acid test* of the profession of the founders. They claimed to be the leaders. Did they lead by word only or by action as well? And to what extent?

This was one area in which, because of the nature of the question, I had to be somewhat negative and look for faults and inconsistencies. I tried to balance that by comparing the record of their lives with their own teachings. That way the pointing finger was their own teachings. I did not have to define what was right or wrong for them. Their writings did that and effectively kept my private evaluations at bay.

I. **Hinduism:** "... When a man gives up all varieties of desire for sense gratification, then he is said to be in pure transcendental consciousness."[1]

   "A person who is not disturbed by the incessant flow of desires ... can alone achieve peace."[2]

   The desires mentioned here are varied but definitely include sensual, sexual desires.

   "Our holy books tell us of gods, sages and heroes who, though high-minded, were addicted to sensuous passions."[3] These were the words of Gautama Buddha when as a Hindu, he reviewed the heroes of the Hindu tradition.

   This is well substantiated in the life of Krishna. His sexual exploits with the "gopi's" (milk-maids) of Vrindavana, of whom Radha was his favorite, is common traditional knowledge. He was even chided by Sisupala for this at a royal meeting "this is not like stealing the clothes of helpless women when they are bathing in the river. This is not like stealing the loves of Gopi women and cheating their husbands."[4] Some sources go so far as to say, "in the course of his life he was supposed to have had 16,108 wives and 180,008 sons."[5]

II. **Buddhism:** "Here venerable gentlemen are the four rules about the offenses which deserve expulsion ... 1) if a monk should have sexual intercourse with anyone."[6]

When Buddha was born, his father, Sudhodana the king of the Gotama Clan was told by a seer that if he wanted his son to be a great world emperor, he would have to keep him from setting his eyes on poverty, old age, disease or death. In an attempt to fulfill his wish, a multi-storied palace was built in which Buddha, then known as Siddhartha, was kept on the upper floors so that he would never come down to the palace grounds and thus come into contact with what was prohibited. To keep his mind occupied, he was kept busy by women minstrels. "They entertained him with wanton swayings ... butterfly kisses and seductive glances. Thus he became a captive of these women who were well-versed in the subject of sensuous enjoyment and indefatigable in sexual pleasure."

"On the night of his renunciation he awoke to find the female musicians sleeping ... some with their bodies wet with trickling phlegm, some with their dress fallen apart so as to plainly disclose their loathsome nakedness."[7] This is a description of a sexual orgy. And this had been going on for day after day, month after month and year after year for at least thirteen years.

During the years of his search for light he said, "I... have gone down to the water punctually thrice before nightfall to wash away the evil within."[8]

His life was flawed according to his own teachings; what he himself called 'evil' was 'within' him.

III. **Islam:** "Then you may marry other women who seem good to you: two, three, or four of them."[9] This is the only place where the number of wives allowed, is spelled out in the Quran. The traditional writings say Muhammad had eleven wives.

"We have given you a glorious victory so that God may forgive your past and future sins."[10]

"Did He not find you in error and guide you?"[11]

Muhammad is acknowledged as the 'perfect man' by Muslim tradition. Obviously this refers to the highest level that a human can possibly attain, 'sins' and 'error' notwithstanding; for, whatever the writings considered 'sins', were found in him. And whatever the degree of guilt, he needed forgiveness for them.

The ideal, as depicted in the writings, was still beyond him.

IV. Judaism: "Thou shalt not kill." "Thou shalt not commit adultery." "Thou shalt not bear false witness."

Moses was guilty of murder. "So he looked this way and that and when he saw no one, he killed him."[12] Later on in the wilderness he expressly disobeyed God who had told him to speak to, and not strike, the rock. This offense was sufficient to keep him from going into the Promised Land, one his most cherished dreams.

Abraham committed adultery. "So he went in to Hagar and she conceived."[13] Hagar was not his wife, Sarah was. This towering patriarch also stumbled at the point of falsehood, when he told a 'white lie' to escape the Egyptians.

David committed adultery. "Then David sent messengers and took her."[14] This refers to Bathsheba who was not his wife. And worse, he had the husband killed in what can only be describes as premeditated, cold-blooded murder.[15]

None of the three Hebrew 'greats' were able to keep their record clean.

V. Christianity: Here are twelve testimonials regarding Jesus.

> 1. Pilate was a Roman Governor. There was no love lost between the Romans and the Jews. Jesus was a Jew. Yet this is what he said, "And indeed having examined Him in your presence, I

have found no fault in this man ..."[16]
"I find no fault in him at all."[17]

2. Herod was a king in the region. Pilate referred to him also as not having found any fault. "Neither did Herod, for I sent you back to him,"[18]

3. Pilate's wife sent him a note during the trial of Jesus cautioning him about the defendant and describing him as "that just man".[19]

4. There was a Roman Centurion at the cross who exclaimed, "Certainly this was a righteous man."[20]

5. One of the felons crucified alongside Jesus turned to another, who was also crucified, and acknowledging their own guilt for which they were being punished, confessed whatever he knew about Jesus saying, "... but this man has done nothing wrong".[21]

These had probably seen him from a distance or had only heard of him. How about those who knew him intimately?

6. John was the closest among the disciples. He had probably watched Jesus closely from morning to evening, day after day for over three years and then decided that "in him there is no sin".[22]

7. Peter was another of the three closest disciples. He too reached the same

conclusion, and portrayed him as "without blemish and without spot".[23]

8. It was probably Paul who compared him to us, "... was in all points tempted as we are, yet without sin"[24]

9. This next disciple, Judas, was apparently disloyal, but after betraying him, confessed "I have sinned by betraying innocent blood".[25]

10. Jesus is the only founder of a world religion who has been acknowledged in the writings of another world religion. He is mentioned ninety-three times in the Quran; multiple times he is identified as the son of Mary and nearly a dozen times he is called the Messiah. In surah 3 and verse 46 [talking of Jesus], "He shall preach to men ... in the prime of manhood and shall lead a righteous life." A significant testimony!

11. The words of Jesus himself were nothing short of startling. Facing bitter opponents who were thirsting for his death he asked, "Which of you convicts me of sin?" The answer was silence. To look within and find nothing wrong is completely foreign to the human experience. Nobody I know has been able to look into his life record to find an absolutely

clean slate. The best of us have such a dismal record that sometimes the very thought of it chokes us with shame and humiliation. Even the highly revered K'ung Ch'iu [more commonly known as Confucius, the founder of Confucianism] confessed, "How dare I claim to be a sage or a benevolent man."[26] In this context the self-conscious purity of Jesus should be taken as a surpassing marvel.

12. The final point refers to the trial of Jesus. In the Hebrew tradition, the Sanhedrin was not only the highest religious authority but also the judicial body making decisions in civil and criminal cases. In small matters, a minimum of three members could make up the quorum to pass judgment. In crucial, major issues, the number was to be twenty-three. When it came to matters of national importance, the 'full council' of seventy plus the Chief Priest was required.[27] There is an indication that the 'full council' had met for the trial of Jesus, but this cannot be clearly verified. However, the descriptions in the story depict a fairly large number. The principle behind the different levels of quorum was to ensure the maximum talent and information, and the less likeli-

hood of judicial blunders, in matters of greater importance.

The trial began with the bringing in of witnesses to see if Jesus could be condemned. As the trial went on it became clearer and clearer that the evidence was not forthcoming; the charges of breaking the law could not be substantiated. It was then that the High Priest himself (going against the law – he was not supposed to play any part in accusing the defendant) examined Jesus. Placing him under the most solemn oath to the Jewish ear, he demanded the answer to the question whether he really claimed to be the Son of God. "Are you then the Son of God?" The answer sent Jesus to his death. The judicial process had yielded a clear sentence of conviction. But the significant point was the shift from deed to identity. The question had moved from what he had or had not done to who he claimed to be. Why the change? Because the whole council, bringing all the evidence it was capable of producing, could find nothing wrong in anything he had ever done. In these judicial proceedings, lies one of the highest forms of evidence of the innocence of this man.

Taking the whole spectrum of testimonials, it is difficult to claim bias or friendship or kinship or any other factor as the basis of the confessions, than the truth about that stainless life. And just like the trial, held so

long ago, which had yielded a clear conviction, so my question now, regarding the life
record of the founders, had yielded an unde-
niable result.

Here alone did I find a life in which the theory
had been perfectly matched in practice; where the
teachings had found their complete fulfillment in
a real-life performance. I had to salute this feat of
an unblemished thirty-three years that had met the
strictest scrutiny from those who had pursued him
to his death. I had to confess that here alone stood
an individual who could look everyone in the eye
and with perfect right and credibility say, "Follow
me." No other founder could legitimately make such
a claim.

REFERENCES

1. Bhagavad-gita 2:55
2. Bhagavad-gita 2:70
3. Buddhist Scriptures, Edward Conze, Penguin Books, 1959, p41
4. Mahabharata, translated by, Kamala Subramaniam, Bharataya Vidya Bhavan, 13th Edition 2004, pp169&170
5. Benjamin Walker, Hindu World, George Allen & Unwin Ltd., London, p561
6. Buddhist Scripture, Penguin Books, Edward Conze, 1959, p 73
7. Buddhist Scriptures p 38
8. Buddhism, The Light Of Asia, KKS Chen, 1968, p 21
9. Quran 4: 2 – 4
10. Quran 48:1
11. Quran 93:6
12. Old Testament, Exodus 2:12
13. Old Testament, Genesis 16:4
14. Old Testament, II Samuel 11:4
15. Old Testament, II Samuel 11:15
16. New Testament, Luke 23:14
17. New Testament, John 18:38
18. New Testament, Luke 23:15
19. New Testament, Matthew 27:19
20. New Testament, Luke 23:47
21. New Testament, Luke 23:41
22. New Testament, I John 3:5
23. New Testament, I Peter 1:19

24. New Testament, Hebrews 4:15
25. New Testament, Matthew 27:4
26. Confucius, The Analects, Penguin Books, 1979, back cover
27. Every Man's Talmud, Abraham Cohen, 1949, pp 300-302

A PAUSE

At this point, I stopped to assess the picture, and it looked too one-sided. This book and this man appeared favored and too dominant.

Was I pushing his story up unfairly and forcing him out to the forefront of the race? Was I choosing only the topics that put them at the top? If I was doing that, it was I who would stand to lose ultimately. I did become a bit uncomfortable.

So I intentionally searched for topics where he would not come out ahead. The next three, [birth, length of ministry, and death] are such. He lands up anywhere but at the head.

CHAPTER IX

BIRTH

Each founder came into this world in an unusual manner. Stories abound regarding those tit-bits that are supposed to point to their status as special individuals.

The Hindu authors did not have many intriguing stories around their births although such descriptions were numerous in the older unverifiable writings, regarding the deities.

Buddha was born after his mother Maya had a white elephant get into her; and when it came time for giving birth, the baby came out in a pain-less manner from the side of her body and not from the birth passage. The first thing the baby did was declare his mission of enlightenment and then take seven steps, with a lotus flower growing out of the ground at every step.

Muhammad was born with a special mark between his shoulder blades that identified his exalted status.

When he was turned over to another family who had the task of nursing him, the milk began to flow miraculously and in copious amounts not only from the 'nurse' but also from their camel which was 'dry' before, but was now able to provide enough nourishment and sustenance for that family.

Moses was born to slaves who placed him in a basket and let it float among the bulrushes in a strategic part of the river Nile where the Pharaoh's daughter came to bathe. She picked him up and took him to the palace and adopted him into her own family. "Moses" means 'drawn out of water'.

Jesus was born to Mary, who claimed to be a virgin despite the pregnancy. The special birth was first announced to some lowly shepherds out on the hillsides who were watching over their sheep at night. A glorious angel suddenly appeared and told of the birth and was immediately joined by a choir of shining beings who sang of God's gift to the human race.

Fascinating accounts, all of them, but I was looking for the points at which Jesus would not be placed higher than the others.

I. **Hinduism:** There is no single person as the founder; there are however multiple authors of their writings. All of them appear to have been revered individuals born to parents with prestige and honor surrounding them.

II. **Buddhism:** Gautama Buddha, known as Siddhartha, was a prince. His father, Suddhodana and his mother, Maya were king and queen of the Gotama clan in northern India. He was born in Lumbini Grove amid great celebrations welcoming the new heir to the throne.[1] His was a stately beginning.

III. **Judaism:** "A man of the house of Levi went and took as wife, a daughter of Levi ... bore a son and she saw that he was a beautiful child ... and he became her (Pharaoh's daughter's) son."[2] The tribe of Levi was a prestigious tribe because it was in charge of the tabernacle, the most sacred possession of the nation. The reputable pedigree was not only in native sense but also by adoption.

IV. **Islam:** Muhammad was the "posthumous son of Abdullah ... his mother Amina ... of the tribe of Quraysh, clan of Hashim."[3] The tribe of Quraysh was not the strongest or largest tribe among the Arabian, but it was very important because it was the guardian of the Kaba the most sacred site in the peninsula. It was a matter of pride and distinction to the family and Muhammad.

V. **Christianity:** "After his mother Mary was betrothed to Joseph, before they came together she was found with child"[4] "... and wrapped him in swaddling cloths, and laid him in a manger, because there was no room in the inn."[5]

Two features become evident.

    a. He was the only founder to be born in poverty-stricken circumstances — among the lowly beasts of the

field, wrapped in cheap, coarse cloth
and laid in a feeding-trough, amid the
stench and squalor of a cattle shed.

b. And worse, he was the only founder
to be born an illegitimate child.

Look over the descriptions of the birth-
stories again. Jesus was the only founder
conceived out of wedlock! In today's world it
may not amount to much but in first-century
Palestine, in that ultra-conservative society,
this was not an acceptable status. It morally
stained the individual as well as the whole
family and was an indication that the favor
of God was not on them. It was a cause for
taunts and jeers. Nor was it something that
he could hide or deny. It dogged his days
from his youth and on through the years of
ministry. In fact, when he went to the temple,
the religious top-brass, and educated elite
dismissed him with disdain, "We were not
born of fornication"! In other words, "Who
are you who pretends to teach the people,
morals and ethics – of all things! You, you
are a bastard[6], we are not! You have no business here among the clean and the favored of
God. Just get out of here!"

How's that for a start in attempting to build a religious tradition! Of all the founders this was certainly
the worst entry, the worst beginning to a religious

cause. On this point Jesus comes out last; last by a long mile.

Yet, some questions remain. How was it that he managed to develop a following despite such a deep, permanent moral stain to his name? Was there something that over-rode this factor?

Another question looms up on reflection: He claimed to be the Son of God. The people, on the other hand, described him as illegitimate because nobody could identify his father in the village or elsewhere. What if the reason was because his father was really God? So, that awful label meant to hound and humiliate, could have been an unwitting admission that his claim might be a possibility. What if the father was really God?! What if ...?

REFERENCES

1. Buddhist Scriptures, Edward Conze, Penguin Books, 1959, p35
2. Old Testament, Exodus 2:1, 10
3. Muhammad, Karen Armstrong, 1992, p19
4. New Testament, Matthew 1:18
5. New Testament, Luke 2:7
6. The word is used in the traditional writings of the Jews. See The New Evidence That Demands a Verdict, Josh McDowell, p304

CHAPTER X

LENGTH OF MINISTRY

The tenure of a leader usually has some reflection on his staying power. This in turn could relate to the way that society in general accepted the person or the teachings. It could also reflect the shrewdness, personality, political power or position, along with any endearing quality that he possessed. We naturally tend to respect those who have been at the helm a long time; the admiration rising as the period lengthens.

How did the founders fare on this point?

I. **Hinduism:** The multiple authors of the various writings lived over a great period of time. Hindu thought developed over many generations. During that time, an organized society was formed with different levels of value for individuals, their birth and parentage, their occupations etc. It turned out to be a vast, complicated system of philosophy and religious practice. This process continued for centuries and then millennia. Today there are close to a billion professors of the Hindu faith.

II. **Islam:** Prophet Muhammad received his first vision in the year 610 CE (Common Era – the same as AD). His last message was given to him in the year of his demise in 632 CE. During those twenty-three years, he gradually, and with tremendous courage and determination, built up a following and an army that not only protected the Muslims but allowed for military conquests which finally resulted in the formation of the mighty Ottoman Empire. It was a combination of religious, political and military power that built the giant edifice for the Muslims. The base was the decades of Muhammad's own contribution in terms of religious and military leadership. Today there is a vast population of over one billion Muslims, with that number growing rapidly.

III. **Buddhism:** After six years of his intensive search for light, Gautama Buddha, at the age of thirty-five began to preach the initial principles of Buddhism. The first sermon was at Varanasi, northern India. His last sermon was given at the age of eighty in Kusinara. Those forty-five years were spent in an extremely active and tireless effort of teaching, preaching and traveling extensively. The later years included organizing the followers into groups called sangha's which formed the foundation of the monasteries that were established to practice and spread the faith. Today there is a string of monasteries over the landmass of south-east Asia and a growing population of 405 million Buddhists.

IV. **Judaism:** Moses began to lead the Children of Israel at the age of eighty and held control till he died at a hundred and twenty. The whole venture was a severe trial for him because the initial group, numbering in the hundreds of thousands, was made up of slaves who had been such for generations. They had no place to call home and so were constantly on the move for forty years, hoping to get to the place they called the 'promised land'. Painstakingly, he molded them, using the principles given him on Mt. Sinai, into an organized nation with specifics religious rites, a civil and health code and a well-trained army. It took the full forty years to transform that rag-tag but idealistic group into a nation governed by precise rules and laws.

V. **Christianity:** The number drastically falls. Jesus traversed the regions of Galilee spreading his message and miracles for a mere three and a half years. This striking difference naturally elicits the question, "Why?" And the answer reveals a truly pathetic picture. His years were cut short by a rejection from his community that was so severe and total that it ended in death.

Let us look at those numbers again. It's not a wide spectrum with Jesus inside there in the middle of the continuum. No, he's at the tail-end. All the founders had decades to develop their thought; enough time, spanning a generation or more to improve, refine and then expound on the message. All of them could look back with a sense of satisfaction on an illustrious career whose influence was changing the very landscape. They had made a statement to the world and it was gaining acceptance everywhere and was clearly taking root in society. Hurrah!

Not so with Jesus. This man had only three and a half years. It was that short because he was booted out, hated with a passion by his community and country, and finally condemned to die as a criminal. There is no question that Jesus comes out last on this point too. Who would be impressed with such a resume!

And yet some questions remain. How long does it take to make a statement to the world – twenty-three to forty-five versus three years? He was only a carpenter-turned-itinerant preacher from a tiny, unknown village in a country that had no political standing except as annexed to another kingdom. His main audience was usually a motley group of fishermen, common folk and curious on-lookers. Why should he be remembered at all, let alone revered and worshiped? Why hasn't time wiped off those short years from history? Others with greater exploits and accomplishments have long since vanished from the horizon. Why the shortest period, the most obscure livelihood and yet now, two thousand years later, with the greatest following the world has ever known?

CHAPTER XI

DEATH

The ending, the coup de grace, of any event or life is nearly always looked upon as a defining moment. There is a certain power that arrests when watching that finale. From the short, hundred-meter dash to the long-drawn-out, grueling marathon, everything along the way recedes into the background when compared to what happens at the tape. The triumph and the pathos; the ecstasy and the disappointment; the making and the breaking, are all focused there. That is where everything seemed to be headed, but we had to wait for that climactic point to see what it really was all about. Always bewitching, always gripping.

I. **Hinduism:** The Hindu masters and sages were revered and held in high esteem. At the culmination of their lives, they and their families were widely praised and honored for the blessing they had brought to the community. Their deaths were regarded as significant losses, to be lamented over for generations, as their lives were recounted over and over again. The masters themselves passed on the baton (of religious thought) with flair, as each expanded upon the labors of the predecessors.

II. **Buddhism:** Gautama died surrounded by his doting disciples who strained to catch every one of his last words. They described the moment vividly, "When the sage entered nirvana, the earth quivered like a ship struck by a squall and fire-brands fell from the sky ... the body was wrapped in one thousand layers of finest Benares cloth and cremated".[1] The cloth was the famed silk from Benares and was meant to portray the highest honor possible. His task was done; he had rounded up his teachings on enlightenment. And now it was left to the followers to continue the good work.

III. **Islam:** When Umar, one of the prominent leaders, heard of Muhammad's demise, he said, "I was dumb-founded ... I fell to the ground."[2] The people hurried ashen-faced to the mosque. The time-honored practice of women beating their breasts was seen throughout the town. Their greatest leader had gone, and, even though grief-stricken, they were going to express their profound respect and admiration. Everywhere were heard words describing that grand and extraordinary life. Muhammad had built the framework for the juggernaut of the caliphate that would later sweep the world and bring almost every opposition to its knees.

VI. Judaism: "Moses was one hundred and twenty ears old when he died ... and the Children of Israel wept for Moses in the plains of Moab for thirty days."[3] The entire nation came to a halt and stayed paralyzed for thirty days. It was a show of great respect, much like when we declare a period of state mourning and fly the national flag at half-mast when a president has died in office. Moses had taken the wandering nation of Israel, the males alone numbering over six hundred thousand, to the brink of the Promised Land; the land 'flowing with milk and honey'. That feat of leadership and organizational skills has remained a marvel to this day.

V. Christianity: "With him were also crucified two robbers, one on his right and the other on his left ... and he was numbered with the transgressors ... At the ninth hour Jesus cried out with a loud voice saying, ' My God, my God, why have you forsaken me.'"[4]

He ended his life stripped stark naked, pinned to an instrument of torture (like the roaches I used to dissect in school), with lacerated skin, bleeding head and limbs, a spear thrust into his torso; rejected and reviled, harassed and humiliated; bearing a

133

gut-wrenching sorrow that finally broke his heart. What a difference. What an incredible contrast! He was not just last in the line; he was in a different line altogether; in a different category – by far the worst!

But the greater the difference, the more the questions that tended to rise.

1. Why was it that when he led, it was by a big margin and then when he lagged behind, he was so far away as to be out of sight?
2. Why would composers of some of the greatest symphonies choose topics from his life as a theme? Were the topics from this criminal so captivating?
3. What made some of the finest artists and sculptors contemplate, and then complete their works with his message as their inspiration?
4. Was there an explanation to the fact that some of the great institutions of learning in scores of countries all over the world started out in his name? Who would want the name of a common criminal to adorn the central structures of those institutions?
5. The largest task-force undertaking humanitarian projects world-wide is the body of people that call themselves by his name. Taken together, throughout history, in all the wars and natural disasters, no other group has been able to match the rapidity, effectiveness, the zeal and self sacrifice of those

who go by that name. What drives them – a condemned criminal dying a horrible death? That wouldn't make much sense, would it?

6. Look at the lengths to which the followers are willing to go. I have seen them with my own eyes – living in huts and hovels, eating the food of those they serve, drinking their water, contracting their diseases, facing the loss of loved ones and babies, and finally dying just like any of the others in those dirty, poverty-stricken villages — unknown and unrecognized, lying today under little mounds of dirt without even a name-tag nearby. What, in the name of anything, causes them to do this? Why point to a naked, tortured body on a cross? Why not to some emperor or military general or some wealthy business tycoon who could guarantee security to the family once they were gone?

7. What if, at the peak of his life, Muhammad was found guilty and condemned to death?

What if Gautama Buddha, near the summit of his life, was convicted and sentenced to hang?

I think such culminations in the story of their lives would have also been the end of all their moral and ethical undertakings. The rank and file would have quickly abandoned them in disappointment and disgust, and we would not have had Islam or Buddhism today.

Jesus was condemned and hanged; his followers left him and fled. Why should there be Christianity today?

8. The Jewish priests specifically demanded death by crucifixion. There appeared a calculated plan behind it. In the books of law, the Torah, in Deuteronomy 21:23, it is written that if the punishment of death was to be by hanging, it would signify that the person had been cursed of God. That body was to be buried before sundown because if left above ground, it would pollute the land — so vile and contemptible was the person. It amounted to incontrovertible evidence of his terrible guilt affirmed by God Himself.

His bitter cry on the cross only further testified to that God-forsaken state.

So, he died a criminal, condemned by the highest religious authority in the nation – the Sanhedrin; by the highest civil and judicial authority in the world – the Romans, and by the highest authority in the universe to the Jewish mind – God.

No noble, lasting cause had ever been birthed at such an ignoble ending of a founder.

Yet, the first converts to Christianity were Jews and some of them were priests.[5] What made those first Jewish priests, well-versed with the Torah, choose to follow him despite such a dismal record? What could have been weightier and more powerful than the pronouncements by the highest religious and civil authorities of his day?

9. No other story has inspired the writing of so much religious literature as the record of this man's life as found in the Gospels. Christian books, periodicals, encyclopedias, poems, verses, songs, research papers etc form the greatest bulk of literary works in the world today, and they are all essentially inspirational, ethical and moral in nature.

   If he ended up as a blasphemer and ultimately forsaken of God, why should anyone listen to and embrace *his* ideas of ethics and morals? The record would have shown how morally bankrupt he really was and this disclosure would have silenced everyone, including those cowardly disciples of his who ran at the first hint of trouble when he was about to be arrested, then later changed their minds and spoke and wrote so boldly about him. Why did they change their minds?

10. If he was just a felon who had finally met a deservedly damned ending to an insignificant, but blasphemous life, why has history been split in two by him – BC (Before Christ) and AD (Anna Domino, meaning The Year Of Our Lord)? What reason to put him in that pivotal position and leave him there for two thousand years? Was there nobody else on the horizons of human history with better credentials than this crucified criminal? "But to believe that a remote impostor, in a forgotten province of a

perished empire, stamped Himself so deeply on Time as to compel all the centuries to bear His name is to believe that a child, with its box of colors could change the tint of all the oceans!"[6]

There has to be more to the story. We must press on to find it.

REFERENCES

1. Buddhist Scriptures, Edward Conze, Penguin Books, 1959, p63
2. Muhammad, Karen Armstrong, 1992, p256
3. Old Testament, Deuteronomy 34:7,8
4. New Testament, Mark 15: 27-34
5. New Testament, Acts 6:7
6. W H Fitchett, The Unrealized Logic Of Religion, p26

CHAPTER XII

POST DEATH

What happened after the founder had died? How was the momentum of the movement sustained?

In most cases there was a tearful farewell followed by the construction of a shrine to keep the memory of the beloved leader alive. The void within the group caused by the death was then filled by choosing another leader so that the movement did not suffer or disappear.

I.   **Hinduism:** There were many leaders and authors spread over generations. What usually followed death was cremation, with great mourning on the one hand, or celebrations with feasting on the other. The remains from the cremation, the ashes, were scattered over and into the River Ganges, the holiest of rivers, signifying a merger with the eternal.

Memorials and shrines then came up in their honor.

II. **Buddhism:** "For some days they worshiped the relics ... with utmost devotion ... divided them into eight parts. One they kept for themselves. The seven others were handed over to the seven kings ... they erected in their capital cities stupas (or memorial mounds) for the relics"[1]

III. **Islam:** "Abu Bakr died after only two years and was succeeded by Umar, then by Uthman. Finally in 656 Ali became the fourth Caliph."[2]

IV. **Judaism:** "So Moses the servant of the Lord died there in the land of Moab ..."[3]

"

> After the death of Moses ... it came to pass that the Lord spoke to Joshua the son of Nun."[4]

VI. **Christianity:** "I am He who lives and was dead, and behold I am alive forevermore Amen. And have the keys of Hades and of death."[5]

> "And lo I am with you always, even to the end of the age."[6]

Weighing these claims honestly, we must confess that the last one, the Christian claim, is nothing less than stunning. Here is an irreconcilable parting of ways between the claims of Jesus and that of any other founder. He claims to be alive after being tortured to death.

Why would anyone make such a far-fetched claim? How would he expect anyone to believe such a report? Truly and bodily alive? After days of being dead? And to add to that, he is said to have predicted it! The first inclination is to dismiss it as a frivolous concoction [a "pernicious superstition" according to the Roman historian Cornelius Tacitus] or relegate it to the level of a chimerical myth. Of all the claims in the universe, this must surely be the hardest to seriously entertain. But we must, at this point, discipline ourselves to remain an inquirer, even if it means going against every grain of rational thought. Yes, it is unbelievable, but it is written in the best attested historical piece of ancient literature in the world and should not be cast away as a myth. That would not be fair. And further, how come so many intelligent, rational, balanced people believe it? What causes them to become so gullible at this one point? Or, do they really have something to go by? But whoever heard of anyone actually being resurrected from the dead?

Once again we find ourselves on the horns of a seemingly unsolvable dilemma: unable to believe it and yet unable to confidently reject it.

Our only hope lies in examining the report the best we can. And here we should first of all, differentiate between an event and the meaning ascribed to it. The meaning that the followers give, is clearly a Christian religious, doctrinal and philosophical point. But the event itself is not religious or doctrinal or philosophical at all. It is a purely neutral, historical claim. "Whether the resurrection of Jesus took place or not is a historical question – and so the question has to be decided on the level of historical argument."[7]

The question assumes huge dimensions and we cannot afford to be lackadaisical and sloppy, for "It is either the greatest miracle or the greatest delusion which history records."[8] We will gain nothing by a half-hearted attempt or one that is predetermined. Here, more than at any other part of our search, we must cling to a seeking, learning attitude; and to help us remain an inquirer we accept Aristotle's pertinent dictum: "The benefit of the doubt is to be given to the document itself, not arrogated by the critic to himself."[9] "One must listen to the claims of the document under analysis, and not assume fraud or error unless the author disqualifies himself by contradictions or known factual inaccuracies."[10]

The event happened two thousand years ago. How much information would there be for us today, to sift and weigh out in a reasonable manner? "Let it be simply said that we know more about the details of the hours immediately before and the actual death of Jesus – than we know about the death of any other one man in all the ancient world – We know more about the burial of the Lord Jesus than we know of the burial of any single character in all of ancient history."[11] From a time and age when written descriptions were extremely sparse, and even single sentences regarding kings and emperors have hardly managed to survive, to find this degree of information regarding an ordinary peasant done to death as a disgraced criminal, is truly astonishing. By today's standards, it might be equal to chapters and chapters of a detailed account. So, we just might have enough in our hands to make an exploration.

The two essential questions that require addressing in an investigation such as ours:

A] If the story is unbelievable, what could the correct story be?
B] If the story is true, are there evidences for it?

A] The Corrected Report

Why attempt to correct the story? Because it is very difficult to believe. It strains our sense of reasoning. We are unable to give a rational explanation for anyone rising up from the dead. I think we should freely acknowledge that. That being the case, any proposed change should fit in smoothly with the rest of the story. It should not leave obvious gaps, unexplained portions and big questions to the point of straining our sense of reasoning; otherwise all we would have done is jumped from the frying pan into the fire.

There have been a few alternatives proposed, but they can be condensed to two basic ones.

1. He did not die – he only fainted (Swoon theory)
2. He died but did not rise – the body was stolen (Theft Theory)
   a) Swoon Theory

The proposal is that Jesus only fainted on the cross and later recuperated because of the cool, reviving atmosphere in the tomb. Does the written story easily allow this suggestion?

i. Pilate's cautious approval: "Pilate marveled that he was already dead; and summoning the centurion, he asked him if he had been dead for some time. So when he found out from the centurion, he granted the body to Joseph."[12] The writer of this Gospel did not know that we were going to ask this question two thousand years later and yet he has given us bits that directly address our concerns:

1. Pilate marveled. Of course he would. The average time from crucifixion to death is days, not hours. Some struggle on for three to seven days before the prolonged ordeal is over. Jesus died in six hours. Pilate therefore wanted to make sure that death had indeed occurred. It would have been a great mockery if the mighty Roman Empire was shown unable to put to death an ordinary Jewish peasant.

2. He granted the body only after confirming death.

3. He was not satisfied with just a quick glance. He specifically asked if he had been dead ' for some time'.

ii. The spear: "When they came to Jesus and saw that he was already dead, they did not break his legs. But one of the soldiers pierced his side with a spear."[13] This was how the centurion made sure he was dead. Realizing that the body made no movement and yet it was too early for death, he was hesitant to bring the body down to be handed over. So he commanded that the issue be firmly settled — with one thrust of a well-trained Roman soldier's spear. If Jesus had not died of crucifixion, he would have certainly died of that thrust because that is what it was meant to accomplish.

iii. Blood and Water: "... the soldier pierced his side with a spear, and immediately blood and water came out. And he who has seen has testified."[14] The description of two streams is what got my attention. Being a physician, I began to look for possible physiological answers. There could be two explanations. One, the blood was mixed with another fluid, like pericardial fluid [produced by the outer lining of the heart], with the blood itself partially clotting so as to remain distinct. Second, the cellular elements of blood, like the Red Blood Corpuscles, settled out to form the red portion, leaving the clear part, the serum, separate. Both these processes require time. Both require that the blood be still and not moving in circulation. The cells do not settle unless the blood is absolutely motionless. This is one basis of a test that some doctors order, called the ESR [Erythrocyte Sedimentation Rate], for which the patient's blood is drawn into a fine tube and kept absolutely still. The doctors usually order a one-hour or a two-hour ESR because it takes time for the cells to settle down to leave the upper portion clear. The spear could have hit at the junction of the two portions thus causing two streams to flow out. The two streams, therefore, could be taken as a fairly strong indication that the blood had stopped flowing 'for some time' – the very confirmation of death that Pilate had wanted before giving his assent regarding the body! The fact that John was no modern-day physician and so described it in the terms of an ordinary layman [water instead of serum], gives great credibility to that simple, specific and yet significant observation.

iv. Multiple testimonials: His own friends, the ones who took him down from the cross, believed him to be dead. That is why they arranged for the burial. If they thought that there was any hope of life remaining they would not have wanted to embalm the body, using substances that would make a return impossible. So, if Pilate, the Roman centurion as well as the friends of Jesus made irrevocable decisions regarding the state of the body, there is no good reason to question it.

v. Escape From The Tomb: Is that a reasonable possibility? His wrist bones were probably fractured, so he could not use his hands. His ankle bones were also fractured, so he could not walk, let alone run. His body had been thrust through with a Roman spear, not a fine sword or javelin. His back was one huge seeping mass of lacerated skin and flesh. If he was still alive, this would have been the time for the wounds to be at maximal swelling and pain. The slightest movement of the wrist, ankles or trunk would have caused excruciating agony. The most he could have done was hoarsely whisper for help.

The 'correct' story should envision that, in this condition, he unwrapped himself from within the tight strips of cloth by an undefined mechanism; found the exact spot of the doorway in the darkness of the tomb; somehow, while still inside the tomb, accurately identified the location of the seal which was on the outside, and broke it; rolled away the stone [called 'golel' which usually requires multiple strong people to move] all by himself, from the inside, and did that without making the slightest sound;

perfectly timed the breaking of the seal and the rolling away of the stone to those exact moments when every guard was 'off-guard' at one and the same time; then hobbled off [none of the guards chasing after him, or able to overtake him] to some location, which, despite the most frantic search, remains unknown to either Jew or Roman to this day.

Have all the questions that naturally arise been satisfactorily explained? Is it easy or difficult to swallow the story that he had only fainted and later had made good his escape by himself?

Reflecting on the above five points, the most reasonable assertion is that, by the time he was brought down from the cross and laid in the tomb, he was dead – dead as a doornail, with no possibility of escape by himself.

b) Theft Theory
   i. The soldier's report: "His disciples came at night and stole him away while we slept."[15] This is one explanation for the empty tomb. But the wording of the report shows that it is a false report. One cannot be asleep and awake at the same time. If they were asleep, how did they know it was the disciples that stole the body? Their testimony stands discredited. If they were awake, why did they allow the theft? They were the ones armed and stationed

there to prevent just this. The report is internally inconsistent. Additionally, the method the disciples used to get into the tomb unnoticed by the posse of professional guards has not yet been outlined. But it does appear to be as improbable as Jesus getting out of the tomb by himself.

ii. Scene of theft: "The handkerchief ... folded together in a place by itself."[16] Neatness is not a feature of a theft scene. The guards were within striking distance. Haste would have been uppermost in their minds and disorderliness is the picture to be expected. Or, were they meaning to get caught red-handed while nonchalantly folding the handkerchief? What could be the explanation for folding clothes!

iii. Naked body: "... Peter ... saw the linen cloths lying by themselves; ..."[17] This was written during the generation that was witness to the events but we have no record of anyone disproving it or even challenging this description. If that is the case, we can deduce that the corrected story should say that the disciples carried away a naked body. The linen cloths were still in the tomb. Significant questions immediately loom up.

1. What were they hoping to accomplish? The tomb and spices were far more than they could ever think of supplying. In other words the

maximum had already been done to show affection and respect. The most honorable gestures had been made. The body had been tenderly wrapped. They probably knew that the women were preparing special spices to embalm the body. What reason can be given for carrying out a naked body?

2. Why waste time unwrapping the body? It would have made better sense if they had just picked up the wrapped body and bolted. It is extremely difficult to find a reason for this time-consuming activity in the face of their intent to steal.

3. Crucifixion was reserved for the most despicable criminals. To strip the victims of every last vestige of dignity and heap on them the ultimate expression of shame, they were crucified stark naked. To claim that these disciples stripped their beloved master and carried out his body completely naked, thus heaping insult on that lifeless form, is to meet a psychological hurdle that cannot be crossed in the conservative, eastern parts of the world – where the event actually occurred. No follower of a revered guru will ever even hint of publicly exposing the nakedness of his master.

This so-called 'correct' story instantly loses credibility.

iv. Soldiers' dereliction: "Therefore command that the tomb be made secure ... lest his disciples ... steal him away ..."[18] The soldiers were placed there at the tomb for only one purpose – to see to it that the disciples did not take the body away. To say that every one of them stopped guarding the tomb at the same time; at the very time when the disciples were at hand; and for the exact length of time required for the disciples to unwrap the body, fold the handkerchief and carry the body to a safe location and out of their jurisdiction, is asking for credulity.

v. Motive for stealing: "For as yet they did not know the Scripture, that He must rise again from the dead."[19] The disciples did not anticipate the resurrection. Even when the story was brought to them they were skeptical. "And their words seemed to them like idle tales, and they did not believe them."[20] They had no reason to steal the body. When their leader was arrested but alive, they denied him and fled out of sheer fright. Is the 'correct' story claiming that after he was tortured to death, the disciples found the courage to rob the body from the tomb, in defiance of the Roman Empire, so that they could proclaim what they knew to be a hoax? It is the presence of the leader that usually inspires and motivates. The death of the leader is supposed to cause depression, discouragement and hopelessness. Here the picture is reversed without an explanation and that does not make much sense.

Looking over these five points, the suggestion of theft by the disciples seems to strain our sense of reasoning and at the same time faces what could be an insurmountable psychological hurdle.

"Non-miraculous explanations of what happened at the empty tomb have to face a cruel choice: either they have to re-write the evidence to suit themselves or they have to accept the fact that they are not consistent with present evidence."[21] The evidence is strongly against the suggestions that he did not die [swoon theory] and that the body was stolen by the disciples [theft theory].

"The difficulties of belief may be great; the absurdities of unbelief are greater."[22]

We should be free to inquire about and consider other options.

B] Evidences for the written story

1. After-effects
2. Eye- witnesses
3. Death-bed confessions

1. After-effects

a. The change in the disciples

"Perhaps the transformation of the disciples of Jesus is the greatest evidence of all for the resurrection."[23]

"A little band of defeated cowards cowering in an upper room one day and a few days later transformed into a company that no persecution could silence."[24]

"They were willing to face arrest, imprisonment, beatings and horrible deaths and not one of them ... recanted of his belief that Christ had risen."[25]

"Think of the psychological absurdity of ... attempting to attribute this dramatic change to nothing more convincing than a miserable fabrication they were trying to foist upon the world. That simply wouldn't make sense."[26]

What could explain the change in the disciples? If they fled from Jesus when he was alive, what caused them to become this bold after he had died? Lying does not make people bold. Truth-telling does. It is falsehood that causes apprehension and fear, especially when aware of the dire consequences of getting exposed. Could it be true that, knowing their whole story to be one colossal hoax, knowing where they had buried that dead body, they deliberately extolled a bag of broken bones and rotting flesh as the 'Prince of Life'; and did it with such intensity, conviction and power that three thousand people, steeped in their own traditions, dropped their life-long, cherished beliefs in one day and decided to follow this man?! Was it really that easy to sell the lie? These people had come to Jerusalem for a Jewish festival and most probably were Jews. They would have known that Jesus had been condemned by the highest religious authority, the Sanhedrin; by the highest civil and judicial authority, Rome; and by the highest universal authority, Jehovah God. There would have to be something greater and weightier than these three factors to make them decide for Jesus. People were amazed at the courage of the disciples. "... when they saw the boldness of Peter and John ... they marveled."[27] The only event that could possibly explain this boldness and also answer to the challenge of the three factors, is the resurrection.

Some think of the disciples as mere gullible fishermen, who grew all starry-eyed about this charlatan masquerading as the Messiah, and with blind, brutish simplicity carried out whatever was commanded them. If they were so bovine, how did they manage to put together such a complex story intertwined with such lofty themes and ideals, maintaining a fair level of consistency in the narration, while expertly covering up all their falsehood in such a manner as to mislead brilliant, analytical minds for over twenty centuries? And if they were so smart as to have accomplished such a feat, how can anyone explain their height of folly in inviting and almost prompting the death sentence, for what they themselves knew to be a complete fabrication? To throw away the deep, basic instinct for self-preservation without proper cause and with such abandonment is a sign of insanity, not intelligence. So, neither gullibility nor smartness is an adequate explanation for the change. However, if the resurrection story was true, neither stupidity nor intelligence would be needed as an explanation. The disciples appeared neither shrewd nor shallow. One inference is still possible – they were truthful.

b. The presence of the Christian Church

This body is the largest in the world and has been in continuous existence since the start. That start involved eleven disciples [after Judas had gone] who wanted to make the number up to twelve [the number Jesus originally had]. In choosing the twelfth member, there were two criteria taken into account. One, the person should have accompanied them all the time, and two, he should be able to bear witness of the resurrection. "Therefore all these men who have accompanied us all the time that the Lord Jesus went in and out among us, beginning from the baptism of John to that day when he was taken up from us, one of these must become witness with us *of his resurrection.*"[28] At its inception, when it was nascent and unadorned, the message was not a new-fangled 'ism' or religion or set of doctrines and teachings. It was the shocking claim that this man had risen from the dead, and they were witnesses to it. Therefore his teachings were to be treated on a different level altogether because they were backed by an event that was unquestionably supernatural. This was the origin and fountainhead of what is now the global body called the Christian church. "The resurrection gave significance to all that they did."[29] Everything else was to be secondary. Around this pivotal point every single utterance would revolve. From this nucleus alone would everything else emerge. Without this, they had nothing to proclaim. With this, they appeared invincible. "Christianity stands or falls with the truth of the resurrection. Once disprove it and you have disposed of Christianity."[30]

Throughout the succeeding centuries, despite adding an immense load of baggage, good and bad; despite detractors by the dozen, the church has remained a real-life entity whose existence cannot be disputed. Tracing it back to its origin, there is only one reasonable cause for its birth and survival – the resurrection. "The institution of the church, then, is a historical phenomenon explained only by Jesus' resurrection."[31]

2. Eye Witnesses

Nobody ever witnessed Gautama Buddha being enlightened under the ficus tree. He made the claim himself. Nobody was present when Muhammad received his many revelations from the Angel Gabriel on Mt. Hira. The authors of the Hindu Scriptures wrote what was handed down to them. They did not experience the actual stories themselves. It is therefore unique to find an ancient narrative written by one who claimed to have experienced and witnessed the events himself or obtained the information from one who had been there. Today's equivalent might be a sworn affidavit. We may find discrepancies and be tempted to question even the whole document, but the basic story cannot be discarded without being extremely unfair and unreasonable. In which of the ancient writings can we hope to find such unequivocal claims by eyewitnesses? Just look at these affirmations:

"Those who from the beginning were eye witnesses."[32]

"... but were eye witnesses of his majesty."[33]

"... he who has seen has testified."[34]

"That which we have heard, which we have seen with our eyes, which we have looked upon and our hands have handled ..."[35]

"This Jesus God raised up, of which we are all witnesses."[36]

"...whom God raised from the dead, of which we are witnesses."[37]

"For we cannot but speak the things which we have seen and heard."[38]

"Him God raised up on the third day and showed Him openly ... even to us who ate and drank with Him after He arose from the dead."[39]

"But God raised Him from the dead. He was seen for many days by those ... who are His witnesses"[40]

"After that He was seen by over five hundred brethren at once, of whom the greater part remain to the present ..."[41]

In other words, at that time, it would have been possible to examine and cross-examine *actual eye witnesses*. Not only did they give their own testimony, they also appealed to the knowledge of the hearers to substantiate their claim:

"Jesus of Nazareth, a Man attested by God to you by miracles, wonders and signs ... as *you yourselves also know* ..."[42] These were the words of Peter to the Jews in Jerusalem

"Why should it be thought incredible by you that God raises the dead? ... For the king before whom I also speak freely, *knows these things* ... since this thing was not done in a corner."[43] This was the claim of Paul before a foreign king, King Agrippa, and it was not refuted by the king. It is quite risky to openly appeal to those who are not exactly friendly, unless the facts are incontrovertible.

How impartial and even-handed would it be to simply toss these statements away without demonstrating deception or falsehood? These are significant words and especially remarkable, coming from a very ancient period when eye-witness accounts were rare. We should be able to give them the weight they deserve. Further, what more data should anyone require before considering the story a possibility? "The very kind of evidence which modern science – and even psychologists, are so insistent upon for determining the reality of any object under consideration is the kind of evidence that we have presented to us in the Gospels regarding the resurrection of the Lord Jesus, namely, the things that are seen with the human eye, touched with the human hand and heard with the human ear. This is what we call empirical evidence."[44] A written statement by an eye witness is one of the strongest evidences to be tabled in a court of law today. Such appears to be the story in the New Testament.

3. Death-bed Confessions

It is generally accepted that somewhere in the back of most minds, even when not explicitly confessed, is the fearful notion of a coming cosmic judgment. Hardened criminals, at the point of death, are known to soften up and become truthful rather than stand the thought of condemnation on that dreadful 'day of reckoning'. This, simply put, is the basis of accepting a death-bed confession as the truth. It is rarely dismissed as falsehood when uttered while facing the specter of death. A death-bed confession from an eyewitness is a powerful form of judicial evidence. If two or three death-bed confessions from eyewitnesses tell the same basic story, the chances of it being nullified by a jury in a court of law are very slim indeed. *The resurrection report is founded on death-bed confessions.* "They were willing to face arrest, imprisonment, beatings and horrible deaths and not one of them ... recanted of his belief that Christ had risen."[45]

Tradition[46] has it that:
Peter was crucified upside down
James was stoned to death
Matthew was killed by the sword
James (son of Alpheus) was crucified
James (son of Zebedee) was killed by the sword
Thaddaeus was shot through with arrows
Bartholomew was crucified
Philip was crucified
Simon the Zealot was crucified
Thomas was killed with the spear
Paul was beheaded

They were not slaughtered together but were sentenced to death, one at a time, over years and decades. There was ample opportunity to reconsider the reasons for their stand. How tempting would have been the thought of confessing the 'truth', regaining their former position in society and returning to the peace and pleasure of their homes and families, if it was all a hoax. Why such horrendous deaths for no cause at all? Imagine dying for 'Alice' who promised a life ' in Wonderland'! That would not stand to reason. One might die for what was *taken* to be truth, but not for what was *known* to be fanciful make-believe.

Multiple death-bed confessions of the same basic story by eyewitnesses cannot be overturned by any fair and just jury.

"Indeed taking all the evidence together, it is not too much to say that there is no historic incident better or more variously supported than the resurrection of Christ."[47]

"On that greatest point we are not merely asked to have faith. In its favor as living truth, there exists such overwhelming evidence, positive and negative, factual and circumstantial, that no intelligent jury in the world could fail to bring in a verdict that the resurrection story is true."[47]

"Thousands and tens of thousands of persons have gone through it piece by piece as carefully as every judge summing up a most important case. I have myself done it many times over, not to persuade others but to satisfy myself ... and I know of no one fact in the history of mankind which is proved by better and fuller evidence of every sort, to the understanding of a fair inquirer, than that Christ died and rose again from the dead."[49]

Arnold Toynbee, studied people who called themselves 'savior' in various times and places. In A Study Of History, Vol 6, p 276, he sums it, "When we set out on this quest we found ourselves moving in the midst of a mighty marching host... In the last stage of all, our motley host of would-be saviours, human and divine, has dwindled to a single company of none but gods ... At the final ordeal of death, few, even of these would-be saviour-gods, have dared to put their title to the test by plunging into the icy river. And now as we stand and gaze with our eyes fixed upon the farther shore, a single figure rises from the flood and straightway fills the whole horizon. There is the Saviour."

"The bones of Abraham, and Muhammad and Buddha and Confucius and Lao Tzu and Zoroaster are still here on earth. Jesus' tomb is empty.

It is the concrete, factual, empirical proof that: life has hope and meaning; love is stronger than death; goodness and power are ultimately allies, not enemies; life wins in the end; God has touched us right here where we are and has defeated our last enemy; we are not cosmic orphans.."[50]

The inquiring mind must bow to the weight of evidence.

REFERENCES

1. Buddhist Scriptures, Edward Conze, Penguin Books, 1959, p65
2. Muhammad, by Karen Armstrong, Harper Collins, p258
3. Old Testament, Deuteronomy 34:6
4. Old Testament, Joshua 1:1
5. New Testament, Revelation 1:18
6. New Testament, Matthew 28:20
7. Wolfhart Pannenberg, Professor, University of Munich in Christianity Today, April 1968, p12
8. Philip Schaff, History Of The Christian Church, 1962, p173
9. Quoted from New Evidence That Demands A Verdict, By Josh McDowell.
10. John Montgomery, in Christianity Today, August 16, 1968
11. Wilbur Smith, Therefore Stand, Baker Book House, 1945, p360
12. New Testament, Mark 15:44,45
13. New Testament, John 19:33, 34
14. New Testament, John 19:35
15. New Testament, Matthew 28:13
16. New Testament, John 20:7
17. New Testament, Luke 24:12
18. New Testament, Matthew 27:64
19. New Testament, John 20:9
20. New Testament, Luke 24: 10, 11

21. Winfried Corduan, No Doubt About It: The Case For Christianity, Quoted in New Evidence That Demands A Verdict, Josh McDowell, p257
22. George Hansen, The Resurrection And The Life, 1911, p24
23. J R W Stott, Basic Christianity, Intervarsity Press,1971, p58,59
24. J N D Anderson, Christianity Today, March 29, 1968, p5,6
25. J Rosscup
26. J N D Anderson
27. New Testament, Acts 4:13
28. New Testament, Acts 1:21, 22
29. LL Morris, quoted in New Evidence That Demands a Verdict, Josh McDowell, p257
30. Michael Green, Man Alive, Intervarsity Press, 1968, p61
31. Josh McDowell, New Evidence That Demands A Verdict, p257
32. New Testament, Luke 1:1-3
33. New Testament, I Peter 1:16
34. New Testament, John 19:35
35. New Testament, I John 1:1
36. New Testament, Acts 2:32
37. New Testament, Acts 3:15
38. New Testament, Acts 4:20
39. New Testament, Acts 10: 40, 41
40. New Testament, Acts 13:30,31
41. New Testament, I Corinthians 15:6
42. New Testament, Acts 2:22
43. New Testament, Acts 26:8, 26

44. Wilbur Smith, Therefore Stand, Baker Book House, 1945, p389, 390
45. J Rosscup, Quoted in New Evidence That Demands A Verdict, Josh McDowell, p270
46. Ralph Muncaster, A Skeptic's Search for God, 2002, p203
47. B F Westcott, Quoted by Paul Little in Know Why You Believe, 1987
48. Lord Darling, Chief Justice of England, Quoted by Michael Green, Man Alive, p53, 54
49. Thomas Arnold, Chairman of Department of Modern History, Oxford University, Quoted by Wilbur Smith, Therefore Stand, Baker Book House, p 425,426
50. Peter Kreeft and Ronald Tacelli, Handbook Of Christian Apologetics, InterVarsity Press, 1994, p177

CONCLUSION

Let us summarize the ten points we have considered and deliberated on:

I.   The New Testament is the best documented ancient writing in the world. It is solidly historical in nature. Despite the scientifically unexplained events recorded, it should not be dismissed as legendary or mythological but examined in a fair manner.

II. The top feature of the Judeo-Christian Scripture, cross-referencing of other authors separated by centuries thus claiming a supervisor who lived the whole period of at least 1400 years, is impressive and has characteristics that are beyond human capability.

III. The Bible's challenge to test it for authenticity is open and clear — the only Scripture with this distinction. And it fulfills its own challenge, predictive prophecy, with amazing accuracy.

These three factors place the writing at the highest level of credibility that any ancient document can hope to reach.

IV. Jesus dared to make the highest claim for himself – Son of God. Because he does not fit into the description of a raving lunatic or an incorrigible liar or a pompous egomaniac, the claim remains a possibility.

V. Jesus did not just explain and expound the truth, the way, the life but claimed to *be* the very essence of them. "I am the way, the truth and the life."

VI. Jesus is the only founder [the only known person on earth] in whom the theory of teaching was perfectly matched by actual practice in life – therefore the only one with the right to say, "Follow Me."

VII. Jesus is the only founder to be of question-able birth and mocked as 'illegitimate'. Yet that epithet could bring in the possibility of his father being out of this world.

VIII. Jesus' ministry was by far the shortest, compared to any other founder, and yet has had the greatest impact.

IX. Jesus is the only founder to die the shameful, violent death of a condemned criminal. This raises a slew of questions regarding the devo-tion granted him by the hundreds of millions even thousands of years later. A criminal managing to split civilized history in two – BC and AD – must be no ordinary criminal.

X. The only founder to go into the domain of death – the most feared enemy of mankind – break the bands and come back as a conqueror over death. And now claims to offer eternal life to "whosoever believes" in him.

These last seven features point to an incomparable claim regarding this man.

Taking all ten together they form a combination that reaches an uncommon mark. Do they constitute absolute proof? No, they don't. I myself can raise questions that cannot be answered. But if I should toss out the whole, it would not serve the purpose of the search. I was looking for something to go by and I found this to be the best. I cannot imagine another claim backed by such an array of solid, open, testable points of evidence. The credibility is of the highest order possible. However, if there is another claim of greater veracity and credibility, I would like to know so I can consider that too. But until such time, will you dear reader, grant me your full and honest permission to follow this man written about in this book? No, I do not demand that you agree. All I ask is that you carefully weigh the evidence and then think, "This person (me) does have a justifiable ground to stand on. His belief does appear reasonable and evidence-based." And once you've said that, then let me challenge you to "Go and find *your* reason to believe."

And may the God of Truth guide you and bring you safely to the harbor of fulfillment and meaning in your life.

What a journey we've had together! What say we meet again!

APPENDIX I

ULTIMATE DESIGN VERSUS AIMLESSNESS

Abbreviations used:　EV = Evolutionism, Naturalism, and Atheism
CR = Creationism, Intelligent Design, Theism

There is a raging controversy between EV and CR that has been going on for generations now, with name-calling, barbs and taunts all thrown in for good measure. Because neither side wants to relent, some attempt to marry the two concepts. When it comes to certain scientific observations, there could be a remote possibility, but on the level of their fundamental claims, they are worlds apart. William Provine of Cornell University, a prominent figure in a prestigious think-tank called CSICP [Committee for the Scientific Investigation of the Claims of the

Paranormal], described the attempt as "intellectually dishonest". Susan Haack, also of CSICP, stated, "I agree with Provine that the hope of reconciliation is ill-founded."[1] I tend to agree with them. Each side piles up a mountain of evidence for itself and then points to the deficiencies of the other and claims that the issue has been settled. Each side ends its arguments with a flourish and finality, "What's left to argue about?"

Here are two statements from the opposing camps, each very confident about its own claims.

"The universe we observe has *precisely* the properties we should expect if there is at bottom, no design, no purpose, no evil, no good, nothing but blind, pitiless indifference."[2]

"... all the seemingly arbitrary and unrelated constants in physics have one strange thing in common – these are *precisely* the values you need if you want to have a universe capable of producing life."[3]

How can 'precise' scientific information lead to such mutually exclusive positions? The answer is really quite simple at this early stage in our discussion. Both EV and CR are not primarily based on observable/scientific facts, but on diametrically opposing world views and philosophies regarding cosmic origins and human existence. True, both have appealed to scientific facts but have interpreted them by their own undergirding principles. So, no matter what the staggering discoveries in science, CR will explain them with, "God made it that way." and no matter how 'mysterious' or 'miraculous' the event or phenomenon, EV will retort with, "Just wait, it will be explained in naturalistic terms eventually." Both can stand whatever argument is brought to them. Both cannot be shown to be false, even if they are. This can happen only in a make-believe world of fiction. But since they are mutually exclusive, reason demands that we accept only one and in doing so we will have discarded the other.

Let's try to clarify the bases.

EV – Every phenomenon is natural. There is nothing super-natural.

CR – God pre-exists everything and created everything – all phenomena.

EV – Unexplained events should be called 'para-normal', because when all the information is in and science has conquered its last frontier, they will all be explained by natural laws alone.

CR – God is without beginning, endless, eternal and infinite. He miraculously created the universe and all life. He holds all laws in His hands and so can produce super-natural phenomena.

EV – The only question is one of time. Wait, all
the answers will come eventually – and
only in naturalistic terms.

CR – The only question is one of recognition.
God is at work in a million places – just
acknowledge the truth of the matter.

The debate continues century after century
because one can start with either proposition and
build a fair case. The other reason is, it is impossible
to directly evaluate and thus prove or disprove either
claim. EV appeals to the future, which is clearly
outside our grasp. CR appeals to the realm of God,
which we are unable to attain.

The only way to decisively settle the controversy
is to get to that ultimate state and from that vantage
point make a pronouncement. But that is plainly
impossible.

We are left with only our own experience and
knowledge within our present sphere of existence.
The piles of evidence are not yet sufficient; the questions still linger. Therefore, I think that, for today,
the debate should include an abstract grappling of the
philosophies themselves, on the level of reason and
common sense. Yes, extrapolating from our present
knowledge in an attempt to explain the Unknown is
fraught with uncertainties; yet we have no option but
to try because (a) The options are mutually exclusive
and we cannot but live under one or the other; and (b)
The choice is not between 'black and white' or 'right
and wrong'; but between 'the most reasonable and
the less reasonable'.

[It is worth reminding ourselves that a 'good' option could turn out 'bad' if we chose the second best while the best was available. Conversely, an apparently 'bad' option (because of the questions that remain) could turn out 'good' if the alternative was worse – absurd and untenable.]

The issue at hand that we are going to consider:

If EV is correct, our existence and that of the universe, originated by random chance and is ultimately purposeless, aimless and useless.

If CR is correct, our existence was conceived in the mind of God and designed with an ultimate purpose and destiny.

After reflecting on these for many hours over many months, I wrote out the points of discussion which follow.

I. Scientists acknowledge that the farthest back one can go theoretically is to one ten million trillion, trillion trillionth of a second; but not to 'zero' time. Alan Rex Sandage, at one time known as the greatest observational cosmologist in the world, said that Science had taken us to the First Event, but cannot take us further to the First Cause.[4] Therefore even Singularity and the Big Bang are post facto. Scientific explanations should not pretend to reach back to 'zero' time. Let's look at one attempted explanation.

"Singularity has no 'around' around it. There is no space for it to occupy, no place for it to be, ... There is no past for it to emerge from. And so, from nothing, our universe begins."[5]

Does this sound like a scientific explanation? Not to me. It appears nothing more than simple guesswork, a mental groping in the dark, and should be permitted to be dismissed by anyone without a second thought.

There is "... the tendency to rescue scientific appearances by evading the mythological point of our science."[6]

EV cannot claim to have an answer. Nothingness is not an answer. It is absence of information, whose equivalent is, "I don't know." Therefore the theory cannot make a statement regarding either purpose or non-purpose. It lacks a basis.

CR claims to have an answer. God, a mind, an Intelligence, is the First Cause. This theory is in a position to postulate that there is ultimate purpose and design. However wrong it might turn out to be, CR has something to offer as an ultimate theory.

II. If the ultimate state is an aimless one, the EV theory is proposing three phases/levels:
    a. Origin – Random, aimless.
    b. Our existence – Abounding in aims and purposes
    c. Ultimate state – Random, aimless.

The focus is on the second phase – our existence. From the cry of a baby for milk to the painstakingly precise work in a space-lab, our activities are shot through with purpose. We perform thousands of purposeful acts. Our whole lives revolve around the notion that only purposeful lives can be a blessing to society. Even an insane individual believes his thoughts and actions to be with good reason. Why would anyone think of proposing any other type of existence?

For the theory to have some credibility there should be an explanation for its proposal. We live immensely purposeful lives (b). There is nothing in observational information to point in any other direction. There seems to be no basis whatsoever for suggesting (a) or (c).

The next question would be regarding the mechanics involved. How did the change occur from the aimless existence of inanimate matter to the purpose seen in human life? Further, What factors will change our 'little' aims in life to make them, at the final count, utterly futile? The answers will have to be arbitrary. It fails as a viable theory, because no explanation can be given for the change from an aimless origin to solid present purpose and then back to ultimate aimlessness.

The CR theory is consistent. There was purpose to begin with; there is purpose today; therefore the ultimate state should be a purposeful one. The extrapolation, from our present circumstance to possible origins and on to the ultimate reality, is a reasonable one.

III. EV claims that given time and a series of discoveries, we will reach a point of being able to explain everything in terms of natural laws alone.

Every fresh bit of information generates its own set of questions that now require more discoveries to be able to provide answers. In other words, we did not even know the questions we needed to ask, prior to the new discovery. "... it seems the more that is known, the more acute the puzzles get."[7] The dictum: the more the facts, the more the questions. Or, The more the known, the more the unknown. Therefore the mysteries and miracles that need explanations are going to only increase in number and magnitude. We are not gaining ground. With each new fact, the hope of explaining everything is receding further and further away. If that is the direction we are headed, the EV claim is only wishful thinking. It is not based on reality.

But just suppose we will come to that point, let's imagine the process. The more we know, the more we know we don't. This will continue till the critical point when we reach the state of maximum unknown – the maximum number of unanswered questions. Then to reach the point of maximum knowledge, the threshold will have to be crossed at that point of maximum ignorance. Then suddenly, presto! What we know will equal all that can possibly be known. No questions will remain.

But, what factor will have caused the crossing over? It cannot be added information because that would bring in added questions. It cannot be a deletion of information, because that would deplete the reservoir of knowledge. In reality there is no such factor. The crossing over is an impossibility. If that state were ever to be reached, we would have gained the status of 'omniscience', all-knowledge, the state of God – the very state that is being denied. The theory cannot sustain itself on reason or logic. It is a fantasy.

Scientists are willing to confess to it. Steven Weinberg (Nobel Laureate) appropriately entitled his book, Dreams of a Final Theory; The Search for the Fundamental Laws of Nature. He is said to have referred to Karl Popper (whom he called the Dean of modern philosophies of science), who suggested that there may not be an ultimate theory for physics. A rival possibility is that such knowledge may simply be beyond us.[8]

EV will have to concede that mysteries will remain; and as long as they do, naturalism will be under question. It could remain as a fanciful possibility, but there would be no basis for converting it into a scientific claim.

VI. Randomness, aimlessness, purposelessness, disorder and chaos do not need an explanation. Indeed, the reason they are described as such is because there is no explanation. If a reason or aim could be ascribed, that event/ phenomenon would no longer be random, chaotic or aimless.

EV claims that ultimately there will be an explanation to everything. This should include our existence. It also claims that ultimately everything is purposeless and aimless, including our existence.

But there cannot be an explanation, which should include aim, reason or purpose, to that which is aimless and purposeless. So, either the ultimate state has an explanation with an aim and purpose, OR it is random and aimless with no explanation possible and none needed. It cannot be both.

If the first, it is a pointer to an Intelligent mind – God.

If the second, it overthrows naturalism which claimed to provide all the explanations. The only alternative to that is CR – God, with ultimate purpose!

V. One way EV discredits ultimate design is to question the existence of God. CR uses the logic that random chance alone will not account for the existence of life. Sir Fred Hoyle, an eminent British astronomer, likened the chances to a Boeing 747 coming together by itself. EV turned the argument around and pointing to the 'Ultimate Boeing

747', meaning God, asked what the chances were of God coming together spontaneously.

The question, on reflection, appears a deliberate approach, to slip slide away rather than enter into a healthy, fair debate.

a. The question is based on EV's idea that God was created at some point. But that is exactly the bone of contention. CR would never call this created entity God. The argument is like shooting arrows and then painting the targets around them; bull's eye at every attempt!

b. The question pre-supposes that there is universal agreement on this point. Nothing could be farther from the truth. This is like demanding to be acknowledged the winner as a prerequisite for the debate.

c. It is both unfair and pitiful, to go over the fence and change the claims of the opponent to suit yourself and then shoot down the touched-up, tailored proposition. CR is very clear and unequivocal that God is without beginning and without end, dwells in infinity, is Omniscient and can hear and respond to millions of people simultaneously. It would amount to creating a 'straw man' if any of these attributes are changed. The correct, fair approach is to show the claim wrong, not change the claim itself. One way would be to show that there is no such thing as Omniscience.

But naturalism would falter and fall if omniscience is not invoked. "When we finally reach the long-hoped-for Theory of Everything, we shall see..."[9] This is an appeal to the state of all-knowledge. The information at that point could explain how to listen to and respond to millions of people simultaneously. But the impossibility of that was used to deny the existence of God. The objection removed, back to God we go! The claim regarding the 'Ultimate Boeing 747' is that it did not need to come together, it always was. This claim has been tampered with because, it appears, that it cannot be, and has not been, overthrown.

"For the scientist who has lived by his faith in the power of reason, the story ends like a bad dream. He has scaled the mountains of ignorance; he is about to conquer the highest peak; as he pulls himself over the final rock, he is greeted by a band of theologians who have been sitting there for centuries."[10]

VI. It is impossible to think of a state in which thought was non-existent. The moment you think of it, thought has entered there. Similarly, you cannot imagine a scene where no imagination exists. For, the moment you have imagined it, imagination has arrived there. If you remove thought and imagination from the scene, you cannot imagine or think of it.

Those who describe the origins of the universe in natural terms, imagine the whole story before writing it down. In that history, life and thought would have to appear at some point. But the writer was there in thought and imagination even before these came to be. That would be a contradiction. One way to reconcile this would be to acknowledge that life and thought always existed, even before Singularity.

> "... where are these laws written into that void? What 'tells' the void that it is pregnant with a possible universe? It would seem that even the void is subject to law, a logic that exists prior to space and time."[11]

Logic requires an active, intelligent mind. There has to be a potential prior to the actual. There should exist, for example, the potential for movement before running can take place. What is the potential, the a priori, for life and thought? There appears to be nothing except life and thought themselves. Since we live and think today, it is reasonable to assume that life and thought always existed, even at or before Singularity.

VII. EV states that once life got going, natural selection sprang into place, took over the process which has resulted in the complex life we observe on earth. The only 'miracle' required was that of life. After that the laws of nature supervened and evolution became a "cumulative one-way street to improvement."[12]

A 'one-way street' is not a description of aimlessness, but denotes direction and therefore purpose and aim. If these were the hallmarks of life right from the word 'go', why should anyone attempt to delete them from a description of the ultimate state and leave it totally aimless and purposeless? The idea is jarring because it is so arbitrary. It is unsatisfying because there is no explanation that can account for such a suggestion. Science has always respected the 'data-to-inference' type of thinking. Where and what is the data for this hypothesis? It is more in line with science to infer that the final, core state of the universe and our existence has purpose and reason, because these permeated the universe from its birth till today.

VIII. Millions of dollars have gone into SETI {Search for Extra-terrestrial Intelligence} because it is just possible that we are not alone in the universe.

What will distinguish an intelligible signal from the crackle and buzz of plain old static? It will have to be a design in the signal. Static has no discernible pattern to it. Whereas if there was, maybe a code, that could be interpreted by laws and rules, the inference would be unmistakable. If that code received from outer space at different locations around the world was decoded and found to contain the equivalent of a whole set of Encyclopedia Britannica, it would amount to incontrovertible evidence of life and intelligence out there. It is a law, a given, that language and communication require life, intelligence and volition.

What if that language and communication is found in 'inner space' like in the DNA of the 75 trillion cells in one human body alone? DNA is an intricately coiled ribbon about six feet in length, packed into a space a million times smaller than the dot at the end of this sentence. It contains enough precisely coded information to fill a whole set of Encyclopedia Britannica. It is not just passive information scribbled on a page. It is a set of complex, non-negotiable, active commands which if disobeyed have dire, if not lethal, consequences. These orders are received, processed and sent out at lightning speed beyond the nuclear boundaries via specific messengers, and affect every part of the body. The process includes coding, decoding, editing, proofreading, adding, deleting, qualifying and quantifying messages. The product is a precision- molecule that is manufactured, packaged, addressed and transported for a specific function, to a specific location where it is unpacked, prepared and fitted into the mechanism there. No human can produce and insert such a mind-boggling apparatus into the nuclei of cells. We must concede the inherent presence of language and commands, submission and obedience to those commands, and therefore of purposes and aims. If this is found in the nuclei of trillions of cells; if those same features are found in the community-lives of hundreds of millions of us Homo sapiens; if we are now ardently hoping to find it among the clusters of gigantic galaxies spread over billions of light years of space, we have effectively encompassed the universe as our horizon. We have acknowledged that there is ultimate purpose everywhere. What will we gain by denying it?

IX. EV claims that the data referred to by CR to describe design can be interpreted differently. If we 'raised our consciousness' we would be able to see that the design that is being claimed is only imaginary. It is only "apparent", an "illusion". There is no design in reality.

What is the difference between 'apparent' and 'real' design? It cannot be in the pattern itself, otherwise there would be universal agreement on the point. To just say 'raise your consciousness' is more like a chant or mantra which could be an illusion itself. The only way to label them as 'apparent' and not real is to prove the designer non-existent. There appears no other way. And those claiming 'real' design must face a similar consideration. The moment 'design' is challenged by the claim of 'apparent design', it should not be touted as fact till the Ultimate is shown to be real.

So, are both the same? They might appear to be dead-locked. But they are not. EV's statement can stand only on reaching the level, and proving the non-existence, of the designer. It is not a deduction based on observation or reason.

CR's statement is based on real observations of design, from which a reasonable deduction was made. How can anyone inspect the mother-board of a computer and the inside of a space-shuttle and claim that there was only 'apparent' design?

On the other hand when there is apparent chaos, there could be design hidden in there. When passing a corn-field, the plants appear scattered at random till a particular point is reached when the design and order in the rows and rows of neatly planted corn become clear. All the other angles showed chaos although there was order always present.

Similarly, once even a single design or pattern is established, the possibility of ultimate design in the face of apparent disorder should be entertained. The terms have to be reversed. It is disorder and randomness that is 'apparent' and therefore an 'illusion'.

X. If the ultimate state is purposeless and aimless, no purpose or aim at any other level or circumstance should matter. Even trying to prove everything aimless, is in itself an aimless endeavor. Whether anyone accepts or rejects aimlessness; accepts or rejects purpose, should make no difference finally. Can there be true purpose in proving or even claiming that everything is ultimately purposeless? If there can be, then everything is not purpose-less. If there cannot be, why do it? For even if it was done just to kill boredom, it would still demonstrate purpose. It is a self-defeating proposition.

The fact is, those who advocate it, exhibit great purpose and aim in trying to explain its validity. They want to be known for their excellence in reasoning it out – and in that very effort, establish the over-riding place of that which they are so keen to deny.

I sense that they do not really believe it but prefer to state it that way for an ulterior motive, aim, purpose!

XI. Ultimate aimlessness means that at the origin of the universe and of life, there was no purpose regarding anything. What then is the explanation for the first organism 'choosing' to live and not die? At least the next generation should have ceased to exist. Dying would not have needed a choice at that primeval stage; living would have required it. The sheer number of living organisms that not only exist but adapt and thrive today should convince us that choice was integral to survival of life. Choice indicates first, a grasp of some degree of knowledge, however rudimentary, and second, the ability to weigh it out before making a decision. Aimlessness cannot discern the essential difference between existing and not existing and so cannot form the basis of a choice. In fact, to choose is to stop being aimless. It cannot account for the trillions of organisms that abound and flourish on earth. The most reasonable theory should involve life, thought and volition even prior to the origins of matter and life.

XII. The principle governing EV theories is, "Given infinite time or infinite opportunities, anything is possible."[13] The statement is scientifically flawed because time is finite. But that aside, I wonder if they really believed it; for if they did, the 'anything' should have included 'God' and 'creation'. But these are strictly excluded, without bothering to address the inconsistency.

The statement is too simplistic and elementary to actually portray anything. With it, neither side wins, although they are opposing and mutually exclusive claims. We are left in the position of the proverbial ass that died of starvation when faced with two equidistant and equally desirable bales of hay because it could not give a single reason for preferring one bale over the other, and so went to neither!

Here's my story of Anything Is Possible.

"The elephant is gone!" the shout rang out in the camp. We all went running to where the elephants were kept. The large enclosure where the bull elephant used to be chained was empty. The bamboo fence facing the jungle was broken, the tall grass and little plants looked stamped upon, and there was the semblance of large footprints leading off into the jungle.

There was a buzz as everyone prepared for the search. But I, being the chief in the camp, stopped them. "It's no use. Let's give up."

"We can get him if we go right away."

"Where will you go looking for him?"

"We'll follow the footprints; they are but a few minutes old."

"He didn't go off into the jungle. We'll never find him."

"Why not?"

"Because a baby ant swallowed him up."

"Baby ant? Don't be silly!"

"I'm not being silly. I did notice a baby ant yesterday, scouting around on that bamboo fence with both its antennae pointing straight to the elephant and with a very hungry look in its eyes."

"Come off it. That's ridiculous. It's impossible!"

"No, it's not. Here's my explanation. Matter is made up of atoms and molecules which are mostly space. If the electrons would stop their endless spinning and settle down together with the protons and neutrons, all that excess space could be eliminated. The difference would be enormous. The matter making up that ponderous creature could easily get into the stomach of a baby ant. In fact, a dozen or more could fit in.

There now, I've produced as scientific an explanation as any. None of you can disprove my theory. None of you can give a more 'scientific' explanation. The question is settled. No more talk. Expedition disbanded!"

There was a rousing round of applause at the exceptional wisdom and leadership I had displayed. Everyone turned to go back to their workstations. But one little girl still had a puzzled look on her face. She was the same one who had earlier lined the streets along with the crowd that was waiting to see the emperor's new clothes and had exclaimed, "But dad, the emperor has no clothes on!" End of story.

Of course, anything is possible. With a broken fence and visible footprints staring us in the face, we are still allowed the freedom to cling to a 'scientific' baby-ant explanation. But it will sound like an "old fashioned folk tale" being told as a "bedtime story" by an "outright crackpot"!

At the level of simple reason and common sense, I think, the gavel must be brought down on the side of Ultimate Design and therefore Ultimate Purpose.

REFERENCES

1. Skeptical Inquirer, Mar/Apr, 2004
2. Richard Dawkins, Oxford Biologist in Science, 277, 1997. [emphasis mine]
3. Patrick Glynn in God: The Evidence. [emphasis mine]
4. Lee Strobel in Case For A Creator, p70
5. Bill Bryson, A Short History Of Nearly Everything, p10
6. Matt Cartmill Duke University Anthropologist, quoted in Icons Of Evolution, Jonathan Wells, p222
7. Nicholas Wade in New York Times, June 2000
8. Bill Bryson in A Short History Of Nearly Everything, p 168
9. Richard Dawkins, The God Delusion, 2006, p144
10. Robert Jastrow (Astronomer) in God and The Astronomers,1978, p116
11. Heinz Pagel, Perfect Symmetry; The Search For The Beginning Of Time, p243
12. Richard Dawkins, The God Delusion, 2006, p141
13. Richard Dawkins, The Blind Watchmaker, WW Norton, 1996, p139

APPENDIX II

RELATIVISM

Relativism versus Absolute truth.
What do these terms mean?

Absolute Truth: There are statements we call facts that are true/valid for all people, in all places and at all times. They could also be called universal truths. They are independent of observation and belief, meaning, whether or not they are observed, whether or not they are believed, they still remain facts and will always be so. All facts are not absolute. Relative truth does exist and has practical application but only when connected to some absolute truth. For example, Mt Everest at 29,000 ft. is the tallest peak in the world, while Kanchenjunga is relatively less in height. This is true despite people's personal opinions and even if it is completely disbelieved.

Relativism: The claim here is that there is no such thing as absolute truth in any sphere of life.

A statement can be true only for certain people, in limited places and at specific times. It is dependent on a variety of factors and conditions including observation and belief. The mind is what gives form and quality. The mind is where reality is created and each mind can produce its own 'truth' or 'fact' from what is observed. For example, Mt Everest can only be said to be the tallest. This report has to be believed and trusted for it to become fact. And even then it could be wrong. Therefore all so-called facts are only relatively true. There is no absolute truth at all.

"... there is no objective standard by which truth may be determined so that truth varies with individuals and circumstances"[1]

"... it will become clear that there is only one principle that can be defended under all circumstances and in all stages of human development. It is the principle: Anything goes."[2]

"... the postmodern world view affirms that this relativity extends beyond our perceptions of truth to its essence: there is no absolute truth; rather, truth is relative to the community in which we participate"[3]

"Foundationalism, the idea that knowledge can be erected on some sort of bedrock of indubitable first principles, has had to be abandoned."[4]

There was no question that Relativism was taking a stand completely against Absolute truth. The gap was unbridgeable. It was one or the other. I had to check it out.

1. The word 'absolute' pictured something rigid, fixed and exclusive, while 'relative' pictured something flexible, easy and inclusive. But on reflection, it was Relativism that was making the exclusive claim – only it was correct and valid, while absolute truth was actually non-existent. The claim was that *all* so-called facts were only relatively true. This exclusive claim seemed to go against its own grain.

2. To the question, 'Is relativism valid universally?' the answer has to be in the affirmative. Asking in another way,' Is Relativism the only truth?' the answer again has to be in the positive and in that very answer, it has established an absolute truth! Relativism has no option but to contradict itself.

3. Relativism claims that a statement can only be relatively true. By that same token, it can also be false. If the statement is regarding Relativism, then it [Relativism] is also false and so cannot claim to be universally true as in the previous point.

4. If Relativism is relatively true as well as relatively false, it depends on another factor, say, my choice, to make it one or the other. If I

choose it [Relativism] to be false every time, it will be absolutely false!

5. To decide whether it is true or false, there has to be a factor, say A that makes it one or the other. But factor A itself is only relatively true and therefore relatively false. We will have to consult factor B to decide whether A has to be taken as true or false. But factor B is no better than factor A, since it is also only relatively true. We will need factor C, then Factor D and on and on ad infinitum! Each step will go further and further away from the original question, that now has no hope of ever being answered. This is called 'infinite regression' – we keep backing away from the questions without answering them. Relativism does not allow answers to be formed or accepted. Therefore, its own answers to questions have no validity. It thus chops the branch on which it is perched.

6. At the point where Relativism is false, its antithesis which is Absolute truth should be true. But Absolute truth dominates completely by its very nature of being absolute. It is not valid for only a portion of the time. Can Absolute truth be wrong regarding the same point at some other times? The absurdity becomes apparent.

7. In this concept, words could have exact opposite meanings. 'Love' could be 'hate' in a relative sense; 'come' relatively 'go'; 'in' relatively 'out'; 'pass' relatively 'fail'

etc., etc. Language would be stripped of its ability to communicate and we might as well be living on different planets or, as Ravi Zacharias says, "in a madhouse"!

8. The word 'relative' suggests a relationship. To be practical and real, one entity has to be set or fixed. For example, where would our place of rendezvous be if we agreed to meet 100 yards to the left of the train, which itself was traveling from Los Angeles to New York at a hundred miles an hour? Relativism is just that practical.

9. In trying to qualify truth and falsehood, the boundaries get blurred. But they are poles apart in essence. Falsehood can masquerade as truth and not vice versa. One can deceive only by falsehood, not by truth. Truth lies within boundaries, all else is false – this cannot be reversed.

   They are made up of different 'substances'. Otherwise, it would be like going to buy a gold bracelet and demanding that it be made of cast iron. What would the composition of the final product be?

10. Relativism must address the other side of the coin, which is 'falsehood'. To be consistent with its stand [which amounts to an oxymoron, because Relativism by definition cannot be consistent], it must claim that falsehood is so only relatively, and is therefore also relatively true. Falsehood could be true! Then, an oath in a court of law could run like this: "I swear

to state falsehood, the whole of falsehood and nothing but falsehood — but Honorable Judge, not to worry, they will all be relatively true." What a travesty that would be!

11. If we agree that there are opposing concepts, we have confessed to the existence of both. For example, to state that something is heavy is to agree that something is also light. If every load on earth were the same weight there would not be any reason to call one 'heavy' or 'light'. So, to claim that truth is relative is to confess that there is truth that is absolute. If even one absolute truth is around, Relativism goes out the window.

12. If everything is relatively true, then everything is relatively false.

13. Relativism is not an axiom. It is a proposition and if so, has to be based on principles of reason and logic. It can be communicated by language only if the words adhere to standard meanings at all times. Relativism, therefore, relies completely on absolute values and yet denies those very values.

14. Paul Feyerabend claimed, "Anything goes". This is the same as "everything is acceptable". If that is what is really being said then, Absolute truth should also be acceptable because it has to be included in the 'everything' or 'anything'. The statement has defeated itself.

15. What have some others said?

a) "So, it looks like any apparent suggestion of relativism is either self-defeating or else is not a real assertion, but something more like an empty slogan."[5]

b) "Most relativists believe that relativism is absolutely true and that everyone should be a relativist. Therein lies the destructive nature of relativism. The relativist stands on the pinnacle of an absolute truth and wants to relativize everything else."[6]

c) "Subjectivism is not an 'ism', not a philosophy. It does not rise to the level of deserving our attention or refutation. Its claim is like 'I itch' not 'I know'"[7]

d) "So if truth were relative, then an impossible would be actual"[8]

e) "Postmodernism's rejection of rational objectivity is self-defeating. It either denies the plausibility of its own position or it presumes the reliability of reason and objectivity of truth"[9]

f) "To assert that 'the truth is that there is no truth' is both self-defeating and arbitrary. For if this statement is true, it is not true, since there is no truth."[10]

g) "To say ' It's true that nothing is true' is intrinsically meaningless nonsense.

The very statement — ' There is no absolute truth' – is an absolute truth."[11]

h) 'We have no compelling reason to accept the theory. We can simply dismiss it as a creative work of extremely cynical people."[12]

i) "The laws of logic must apply to reality; else we may as well be living in a madhouse"[13]

j) "A mood can be a dangerous state of mind, because it can crush reason... But that is precisely what I believe postmodernism best represents – a mood."[14]

k) By way of summary, here's an anecdote.

"A friend of mine told me that when Christian apologist and author Ravi Zacharias visited Columbus to speak at Ohio State University, his hosts took him to visit the Wexner Center for the Arts. The Wexner Center is a citadel of postmodern architecture. It has stairways leading nowhere, columns that come down but never touch the floor, beams and galleries going everywhere, and a crazy-looking exposed girder system over most of the outside. Like most of postmodernism, it defies every cannon of common sense and every law of rationality.

Zacharias looked at the building and cocked his head. With a grin he asked, ' I wonder if they used the same techniques when they laid the foundation?'

His point is very good. It's one thing to declare independence from reality when building a monument. It's another thing when we have to come into contact with the real world."[15]

Relativism was not a philosophy, not an 'ism'. It was full of contradictions and phantom-like as to its real nature. It was more like a 'slogan' or a 'mood'. It would be suicidal to base any of my major decisions on it. It was out for the count.

REFERENCES

1. David Trueblood, Philosophy of Religion, 1957, p348
2. Paul Feyerabend, quoted in New Evidence, Josh McDowell, p617
3. Stanley Grenz, Primer on Post Modernism, 1996, p8
4. Millard Erickson, quoted in New Evidence, Josh McDowell, p617
5. Michael Jubien, Contemporary Metaphysics, 1997, p89
6. Norman Geisler
7. Peter Kreeft, Handbook of Christian Apologetics, 1994, p372
8. Norman Geisler
9. Dennis McCallum, The Death of Truth, 1996, p53
10. William Craig, quoted in New Evidence, Josh McDowell, p620
11. Gene Veith, Post Modern Times, 1994, p16
12. Dennis McCallum, The Death of Truth, 1996, p53
13. Ravi Zacharias, Can Man Live Without God, p11
14. Ravi Zacharias, Jesus Among Other Gods, pvii
15. McCallum in The Real Issue, quoted in New Evidence, Josh McDowell, p620

APPENDIX III

PLURALISM

I n trying to clarify the idea of Pluralism, I drew a diagram like the one below.

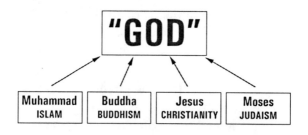

On seeing it, a friend exclaimed, "That's exactly what I believe!"

"And why so?" I asked.

"Well, I think that when anybody worships or prays to or thinks about 'God', the name may be different but that Supreme Being is the same."

"Then you do not claim to hold to any religion?"

"Actually, I'm a Buddhist. But I believe everyone's religion be it Hinduism, Christianity or Islam, leads to the same Ultimate Being, just like in your drawing. I can't see how anyone can claim this or that to be the only correct one."

"Does the Buddhist literature ever state that Brahma, Vishnu etc. along with Buddha lead to this Ultimate Being?"

"Hmmm... I guess not."

I found this idea of 'all roads leading to Rome' espoused by the majority. Sometimes it was not an open claim, just a lingering suspicion in the back of the mind, even among those professing their faith very strongly.

"When Jews or Muslims, for example, praise God as Creator of the world, it is obvious that they are referring to the same Being. We may assume that they are intending to worship the one Creator God that we also serve... If people in Ghana speak of a transcendent God ... how can anyone conclude otherwise than that they intend to acknowledge the true God as we do?"[1]

"Of course Buddhism is not Christianity and does not try to be. But how does one come away after encountering Buddhism and deny that it is in touch with God in its way,"[1]

"God is in the world – but Buddha, Jesus, Muhammad are in their little closets, and we should thank them but never return to them."[2]

"To understand God is to listen. Listen to Jesus and Muhammad and Buddha, but don't get caught up in the names. Listen beyond them; listen to God's breath."[3]

".. Pluralism – recognizes not only the existence of other religions but their intrinsic equal values."[4]

Whenever I asked if this was found in their written literature, there was hesitancy first, then a slow acknowledgment that it was not there. So, I went to the various scriptures to see what really was there.

HINDUISM:

"I am the goal, the upholder, the master, the witness, the home, the shelter and the most dear friend. I am the creation and the annihilation, the basis of Everything, the resting place and the eternal seed."[5]

'Let there be one scripture... for the whole world – Bhagavad-gita; Let there be one God for the whole world – Sri Krishna: one hymn, one mantra, one prayer— the chanting of his name."[6]

ISLAM:

"Allah! There is no God but He – The Living, The Self-subsisting, Supporter of all – His are all things in the heavens and on earth— His throne doth extend over the earth – He is the Most High, The Supreme"[7]

"Verily I am Allah; There is no God but I."[8]

BUDDHISM:

"This Lord is truly the Arhat, fully enlightened, perfect in his knowledge and conduct, well-gone, world-knower, unsurpassed, leader of men to be tamed, teacher of gods and men, the Buddha, the Lord."[9]

JUDAISM:

"For thus saith the Lord, who created the heavens, who is God, who formed the earth – I am the Lord and there is no other."[10]

"I have sworn by Myself; The word has gone out of my mouth in righteousness, and shall not return, that to Me every knee shall bow."[11]

CHRISTIANITY:

> "For there is no other name under heaven, given among men by which we must be saved."[12]

> "I am the Way, the Truth and the Life. No one comes to the Father except through Me."[13]

These statements were unequivocal, sharp and very clear. There was no ambiguity at all. No, I did not find in any of the writings the sanction that the other religions were a good, equal alternative.

> "In a broad sense all religious traditions are exclucivist, inasmuch as they maintain their central affirmations to be true."[14]

> "The exclusive claim has long been assumed on all hands. Even Hinduism which with some justice prides itself on a hospitable stance is, from that angle just as rejectionist of Semitic instincts as it sees them to be"[15]

> "At the heart of every religion is an uncompromising commitment to a particular way of defining who God is or is not and accordingly, of defining life's purpose... Every religion at its core is exclusive."[16]

> "What is truly arrogant is the postmodernist pluralism which, in vain pursuit of a superfi-

cial tolerance, negotiates away the ultimate commitment by which any religion lives."[4]

"Agreement... cannot be made without substantial compromise of core beliefs."[17]

There was a severe clash between the sacred writings and the claims of Pluralism. Both could not be valid, in fact they were mutually exclusive. I would have to examine Pluralism.

1. Exclusivism came 'ready made', inherent in the written codes. Pluralism, on the other hand was a development. It had to be built up from scratch and could claim, as its basis, only opinions and suppositions from various individuals. And all they were trying to do was explain the writings. The problem was that the explanations were going contrary to the written claims.

2. To show necessity for change, evidence must be provided that the old was deficient, irrelevant, defunct or false. But Pluralism could not claim to find irrelevancy or falsehood and yet say that they were all equally valid and true. To find anything to change would be to make Pluralism irrelevant. The need would be to fix that problem and not bring in Pluralism.

3. The claim of equality presupposes a universally acceptable reference point. If two people claimed to be the same weight, they

should have gone to the same weighing machine. But there is no such reference point for religion. How can civilized society accept that voodooism and witchcraft and child sacrifice are equal to Buddhism or Islam or Christianity?

4. To replace anything, the authority over that jurisdiction has to be established. The religions themselves held independent authority within the religion and the body of believers and they clearly claimed exclusivity. Pluralism had only a derived, second-hand one, if any, and therefore was not in a position to overturn any claim of the religions.

5. If Pluralism claimed to oppose only the principle of exclusivism and not the religions themselves, it would have to show evidence that the religions did not claim that position. But the writings were too clear; they were claiming exclusivity and so, Pluralism was definitely challenging the religions, at least, on that point. It was questioning the truth of their claims and yet saying that they were all correct. You can't 'have your cake and eat it'!

6. The religions claimed that their information came from a supernatural source and was brought to us humans accompanied by unusual,' miraculous' phenomena. This is what authenticated their status as super-human. There was nothing in Pluralism to

match this. It was only an opinion with just that much weight to its claim.

7. The Zen saying asked us to listen *to* the founders and also to listen *beyond* them. The problem arose when you really attempted that, because when you listened *to* them, they were unquestionably decided that you should never listen *beyond* them to anyone else. For example, if you listened *to* Muhammad, he would emphatically tell you not to listen *beyond* him. So, we have a choice to either listen to them or beyond them. It is not possible to do both. The Zen saying is not practical.

8. To be really serious in matters of eternal consequences, there should be a clear promise of rewards on compliance and an equally clear description of the consequences of non-compliance. Furthermore, since this would involve detailed, unerring judgments, the power and ability of that source would become extremely important questions. There should be a claim that no mistakes would be made; the final judgments would be infallible. Pluralism had nothing to back itself on this point.

9. If even one religion claimed to be exclusively correct, then to leave them all as before and yet that they were all equal, was to give them equal as well as exclusive status at one and the same time. This would not be a logical or

practical stand. Either exclusivity or equality, but not both.

10. If we acknowledge that all religions lead to the same 'God' and retain the fact that this 'God' gave each its exclusive stand, this 'God' could be called a liar and a devious One too. He told the Hindu's about their numerous deities and then struck that whole concept down with Muhammad's fiercely monotheistic declaration. 'God' reveled in this duplicity, pitting one against every other, creating strife and animosity down through the ages. The worst wars in history were 'religious' wars! Pluralism has to own up to this concept of 'God'.

11. Proper names are a precise form of identification, and once given, society demands that we respect that identification as distinct. Of course many people can have the same name and one person can have many names, aliases. Pluralism refers to this 'God' with many names. The plea is that since there are many similarities, the reference is probably to the same Ultimate Being.

But similarities are not as much the deciding factors as are differences. If we found 100,000 similarities between two complex organisms, would it make a difference if one's name was Adolf Hitler and the other's was Mother Teresa? *Even one irreconcilable difference* will negate all the similarities to be found.

Allah is the proper *name* of God in Arabic.

Jesus is the *"name"* given among men.

Aliases could be a possibility but not once in the Bible is Allah an alias for Jehovah or Jesus and not once in the Quran is Buddha or Vishnu an alias for Allah. Not Once!

With reference to my diagram, there is no 'God' above Allah or Jesus or Brahma. Nobody has yet demonstrated the authority or the rationale to change these names to a generic form.

12. To introduce and sustain Pluralism, the initial requirement is to go to the founders Muhammad, Jesus, Moses etc and show them to be wrong, bigoted and intolerant. Whatever method is used, the attempt will end up in complete despair or in mutilating the religions to a point beyond recognition. All that will be left will be a heap of garbled, incoherent, meaningless utterances for which you can give neither rhyme nor reason. Try it and see for yourself.

13. It is not possible to follow all the religions at the same time. One religion or portions of different ones may be possible. So, could an individual choose any part of any religion, at random, to make up a set of beliefs? But that would be forming a new religion and this new one would take its place among the others, just like the others before. The round of questions

would start all over again. Making circles is not a sign of progress.

Furthermore, a new 'God' would be needed. But a 'manufactured' God would have no inherent power or position; only that which the individual has seen fit to bestow. Who would be dominant – 'God' or the individual?

14. The religions not only claimed exclusivity, they pointed to the drawbacks of others.

"The Buddha held that this belief in a permanent self or soul is one of the most deceitful delusions ever held by man"[18]. He was referring to the core teaching of the Hindu's.

"All who ever came before Me are thieves and robbers"[19]. These are the words of Jesus.

"... are like a donkey laden with books. Wretched is the example of those who deny God's revelations"[20]. This is a statement from the Quran, referring to the Jews and Christians

Statements such as these make it impossible for Pluralism to maintain the concept that they all are equally valid, good and credible, and therefore acceptable.

15. There is an illustration that keeps making the rounds whenever this topic comes up. It is the story of the King's elephant that three blind men felt and described. One felt the tail and said the elephant was like a brush. The one whose arms circled the leg called it a tree.

The one who played with the trunk pictured it as a pipe. So, in the religious world, each religion is but a part of the whole and people are able to describe and advocate only portions of the actual whole. Nobody should ever claim that theirs is the only and last word on the subject.

It sounds good until it is questioned. The three blind persons represent the whole of humanity. Then who is the king and who is the story-teller? If they are not of this world, what is their identity? How did the reporter know that there was a king and an elephant? If they are part of humanity, how did they escape the universal blindness so as to be able to see the elephant and the other blind people?

The king or the reporter is actually non-existent. Therefore any report is a fabricated one, or from just another blind person who cannot claim to have seen the elephant. The illustration lacks a fundamental basis.

It is more reasonable to opine that we all have tunnel-vision and are able to appreciate only certain narrow, limited values. The brush, the tree and the pipe are different entities, just like the different religions, and each is claiming to be the truth. There is no basis of saying that they all ultimately belong to one identity – one generic religion.

16. Pluralism takes a cue from another common expression, "All roads lead to Rome". Thus the claim, that all religions are only different paths to the same final destination.

During the days of the Roman Empire, the roads did not start out in the periphery. The roads were built centrally first and then went out in all directions. In other words, the destination came first and preceded the network of roads. This cannot be said of religious endeavors. Our starting point and the direction of progress is exactly the opposite. We have not reached the destination. And that brings us to the most crucial observation. Rome was established in the minds of people as real, concrete and well-known. There was universal agreement regarding this reality. Once in Rome, one could observe the fact that all the roads were leading there. The various travelers coming in and going out could also vouch for it. The expression was valid only because of this. Without a real Rome; without real journeys to and from that real destination, there would be nothing to back the expression. Likewise, in the case of religions, this expression of Pluralism would be valid only if the destination had been actually reached from different paths coming from different directions. But truth be told, there is no universal agreement regarding the destination. We cannot vouch for anything about it, let alone its relationship to every road. Then, what is the basis of saying that these roads actually reach there? Can there be any other way of validating the claim? No, indeed there cannot! None of those who make the claim have been to the destination and back. Alas, then, the base, the foundation is absent. The claim has lost touch with reality.

Pluralism is nothing more than wishful thinking. It is not found in the sacred writings. Its reasons do not stand scrutiny. As an honest inquirer, I must lay it aside and prefer the clear, exclusive claim of each religion.

REFERENCES

1. Pinnock
2. W.E. Hock
3. A Zen Saying
4. Timothy George
5. Bhagavad -gita 9:18
6. Introduction to the Bhagavad-gita
7. Quran 2:255
8. Quran 20:14
9. Buddhist Scriptures
10. Old Testament, Isaiah 45:18
11. Old Testament, Isaiah 45:23
12. New Testament, Acts 4:12
13. New Testament, John 11:24
14. Ramesh Richard
15. Cragg
16. Ravi Zacharias
17. Paul Marshall et al
18. Buddhism The Light of Asia, KKS Chen, 1968, p44
19. New Testament, John 10:8
20. Quran 62:5

BIBLIOGRAPHY

1. Buddhism, The Light Of Asia by KKS Chen, Barron's Educational Series Inc, 1968
2. Buddhist Scriptures, Translated by Edward Conze, Penguin Books, 1959
3. Mahabharata, Translated by Kamala Subramaniam, Bharatiya Vidya Bhavan, 2004
4. Bhagavad-gita As It Is, AC Bhaktivedanta Swami Prabhupad, Bhaktivedanta Book Trust, 1986
5. The Bible, New King James Version, Thomas Nelson Inc, 1979
6. The Quran, Translated by NJ Dawood, Penguin Books, 2000
7. Muhammad, Karen Armstrong, Harper SanFrancisco, 1992
8. Every Man's Talmud, Abraham Cohen, Schocken Books, 1949
9. The New Evidence That Demands A Verdict, Josh McDowell, Thomas Nelson Publishers, 1999

10. Jesus Among Other Gods, Ravi Zacharias, W Publishing Group, 2000
11. A Skeptic's Search For God, Ralph Muncaster, Harvest House Publishers, 2002
12. The Case For A Creator, Lee Strobel, Zondervan, 2004
13. Icons Of Evolution, Jonathan Wells, Regnery Publishing, 2000
14. But Don't All Religions Lead To God?, Michael Green, Baker Books, 2002

Printed in the United States
117561LV00001BB/133-699/P

9 781606 473634